Sentence Composing
for Middle School

A Worktext on Sentence Variety and Maturity

Don Killgallon

Boynton/Cook Publishers
Heinemann
Portsmouth, NH

To Jen, for coaching, cheering, and often
carrying the ball.

Boynton/Cook Publishers
361 Hanover Street
Portsmouth, NH 03801-3912

Offices and agents throughout the world

Library of Congress Cataloging-in-Publication Data
Killgallon, Don.
    Sentence composing for middle school : a worktext on sentence
variety and maturity / Don Killgallon.
        p.   cm.
    Includes bibliographical references.
    ISBN 0-86709-419-2 (alk. paper)
    1. English languge—Sentences—Study and teaching (Elementary)
2. English language—Composition and exercises—Study and teaching
(Elementary)   I. Title.
LB1576.K485   1997
372.62'3—dc21   97-27433
                                                                      CIP

Acquisitions editor: Peter Stillman
Production editor: Renée Nicholls
Cover designer: Jenny Jensen Greenleaf
Manufacturing coordinator: Louise Richardson

Printed in the United States of America on acid-free paper
    10 ML 19

Contents

Preface

This series—*Sentence Composing for Middle School, High School, and College*—emphasizes the most neglected unit of written composition: the sentence. Using four sentence-manipulating techniques—*sentence scrambling, sentence imitating, sentence combining,* and *sentence expanding*—these books teach students structures they seldom use in their writing but should, and can easily use once they become familiar with them through many examples and practices.

Each book concentrates on such structures, by means of model sentences by professional writers. The rationale is based on the widely accepted mimetic theory of oral language acquisition, applied here to written language acquisition, in the belief that continual exposure to structures used often by professionals in their sentences will produce attention to, understanding of, and, with practice, normal use of such structures by students in their sentences.

The books are exercises in applied grammar, with the theory and terminology of grammar subordinate to the major goal: composing sentences. The naming of parts and the parsing of sentences, the goals of traditional grammar study, are exercises in dissection. The practices in *Sentence Composing* are exercises in production.

The sentence-manipulating techniques are easily learned. The practices based on them are interesting and challenging, and they can be done by any student. In addition, the teacher can readily give attention to the sentences students compose, with quicker, more constant, and more thorough feedback than with longer compositions.

Since the practices have proved successful for the great majority of students who have used them in all kinds of schools, it is demonstrably true that *Sentence Composing* can work anywhere, in any school, with any student.

DON KILLGALLON
Baltimore, Maryland

v

Introduction

How Sentence Composing Works

When you or a professional write, you both choose words and arrange them in sentences, but often with very different results: variety and maturity in sentences written by professional writers are much more evident than in sentences written by students. Unlike professional writers, students tend to write sentences similar to sentences they speak.

The big difference in variety and maturity is what this worktext is all about. The idea of *sentence composing* is to bridge that gap, so that your sentences more closely resemble in structure those written by professional writers. Throughout the worktext, you will see how professional writers write their sentences. You will learn and practice writing similar sentences by using four easy-to-learn techniques: *sentence unscrambling, sentence imitating, sentence combining,* and *sentence expanding.*

You will learn by imitating the pros. Just as you used imitation as a child to learn to speak by imitating experienced speakers like your parents, you can learn to write better sentences by imitating how professional writers use written language.

Nothing in the worktext is difficult to learn. You don't have to know a lot about grammar. You don't have to learn lots of terms. You don't have to study to take tests. But you do have to want to improve the sentences you write. This worktext will show you how.

First you have to learn something, and then you can go out and do it.
Mies van der Rohe

How to Use This Worktext

All practices in this worktext use model sentences written by professional writers. Throughout the worktext you will practice sentence unscrambling, sentence imitating, sentence combining, and sentence expanding to learn to write sentences that have the kind of variety and maturity in the model sentences.

You can learn a lot about writing in general through the practices in this worktext, not just about how professionals write their sentences. Even though you will be working with sentences—the backbone of all writing—you can learn skills that will help you improve any kind of writing: paragraphs, essays, short stories, reports, and research papers.

The References section at the end of the worktext contains the original sentences by professional writers used as models in the practices throughout the worktext. Don't consider them the answers in the back of the book, as in a math textbook.

When you look up the original sentences you may decide that the professionally written sentence is better than yours; if so, study the difference. You may, however, decide that yours is just as good; if so, congratulate yourself. You may even decide that yours is better; in that case, take a bow.

1

Sentence Unscrambling

In this part of the worktext, you will learn how to arrange sentence parts effectively within a sentence by unscrambling lists of sentence parts.

All of the sentences you will unscramble were written by professional writers. In unscrambling their sentences, pay attention to how they composed their sentences. Apply what you learn to your own sentences.

Activity 1

Understanding Sentence Parts

Practice 1

People read and write in sentence parts, that is, chunks of meaning. In one sentence below, sentence parts are divided into meaningful chunks. In the other, they are divided meaninglessly. Try reading both sentences. Identify the one that's easier to read because sentence parts are divided into meaningful chunks.

1. Tobacco is a / custom loathsome to / the eye hateful to the nose harmful / to the brain dangerous / to the lungs and in the / black stinking fume thereof nearest / resembling the horrible / smoke of / the pit that is / bottomless.

2. Tobacco is a custom / loathsome to the eye / hateful to the nose / harmful to the brain / dangerous to the lungs / and in the black stinking fume thereof / nearest resembling / the horrible smoke / of the pit / that is bottomless.

    James I, "A Counterblast to Tobacco"

Practice 2

Read each pair of sentences, pausing at the slash lines, and then identify the sentence that is divided into meaningful chunks (sentence parts).

1a. I am not / ashamed to confess that / I am / ignorant of what I / do not know.

 b. I am not ashamed / to confess / that I am ignorant / of what I do not know.

    Cicero

2a. If you / put a chain around the / neck of a / slave the other / end fastens / itself around your own.

b. If you put a chain / around the neck / of a slave / the other end / fastens itself / around your own.

Ralph Waldo Emerson, "Compensation"

3a. If a man bites / a dog that / is news.

b. If a man / bites a dog / that is news.

John Bogart

4a. A pessimist / is one who feels bad / when he feels good / for fear he'll feel worse / when he feels better.

b. A pessimist is one who feels / bad when he / feels good for / fear he'll feel / worse when he feels better.

Anonymous

5a. Optimism is a / cheerful frame of / mind that enables a tea / kettle to sing though / in hot water up / to its nose.

b. Optimism is / a cheerful frame of mind / that enables a tea kettle / to sing / though in hot water / up to its nose.

Anonymous

6a. There are three marks / of a superior man / being virtuous / he is free from anxiety / being wise / he is free from perplexity / being brave / he is free from fear.

b. There are three marks of a superior man being / virtuous he is free / from anxiety being wise / he is free from perplexity being brave / he is free from fear.

Confucius

7a. To have and to hold from this day forward for better / or for worse for richer / or for poorer in sickness / and in health to love / and to cherish till death / do us part.

b. To have and to hold / from this day forward / for better or for worse / for richer or for poorer / in sickness and in health / to love and to cherish / till death do us part.

Book of Common Prayer

8a. The only way / to keep your health / is to eat what you don't want / drink what you don't like / and do what you'd rather not.

b. The only way to / keep your health is to eat what / you
   don't want drink / what you don't like and do what you'd /
   rather not.

Mark Twain

9a. There are three ways / to get something done do / it
    yourself hire / someone or forbid your / kids to do it.

b. There are three ways / to get something done / do it
   yourself / hire someone / or forbid your kids to do it.

Monta Crane

10a. Perhaps the most / valuable result of all / education is the
     ability to make / yourself do the thing you / have to do
     when it ought to be done whether / you like it or not.

b. Perhaps the most valuable result / of all education / is the
   ability / to make yourself do the thing you have to do /
   when it ought to be done / whether you like it or not.

Thomas Henry Huxley

*A*ctivity 2

Identifying Sentence Parts

Practice 1

The sentence parts below are chunked meaninglessly. Copy the sentences and reposition the slash lines to make meaningful chunks.

1. When fate hands / you a lemon try to / make lemonade.
   Dale Carnegie

2. Even if it's a little / thing do something for / others something for / which you get no pay but / the privilege of doing it.
   Albert Schweitzer

3. The best / way to / cheer yourself up is to / try to cheer somebody else up.
   Mark Twain

4. A sentence should contain no / unnecessary words a paragraph no unnecessary / sentences for the same reason that a / drawing should have no unnecessary lines and a / machine no unnecessary parts.
   William Strunk

5. Always be nice to / people on the way up because you'll / meet the same people on / the way down.
   Wilson Mizner

6. When you have a / number of disagreeable / duties to perform / always do the most / disagreeable first.
   Josiah Quincy

7. Keep five yards from a carriage ten / yards from a horse and a hundred / yards from an elephant but the / distance you should keep from a wicked / person cannot be measured.
   Indian proverb

8. Ask not what your / country can do for / you but ask what you can / do for your country.
   President John F. Kennedy

9. You can make more / friends in two months by becoming interested in other people than / you can in two / years by trying to get other / people interested in you.

Dale Carnegie

10. If you wish to / rest first work.

Anonymous

Practice 2

Copy each sentence twice. The first time, insert slash lines in meaningless places. The second time, use the same number of slash lines for meaningful sentence parts.

1. A politician thinks of the next election a statesman of the next generation.

James Freeman Clarke

2. A politician is an animal who can sit on a fence and yet keep both ears to the ground.

Anonymous

3. It is of great importance in a republic not only to guard against the oppression of its rulers but to guard one part of society against the injustice of the other part.

Alexander Hamilton

4. In a free country there is much clamor with little suffering in a despotic state there is little complaint with much grievance.

Lazare Carnot

5. Those who deny freedom to others deserve it not for themselves and under a just God cannot long retain it.

Abraham Lincoln

6. I would rather sit on a pumpkin and have it all to myself than to be crowded on a velvet cushion.

Henry David Thoreau

7. If you would not be forgotten as soon as you are dead either write things worth reading or do things worth writing.

Benjamin Franklin

8. If you want to get along go along.

Sam Rayburn

9. Never do today what you can put off till tomorrow because delay may give clearer light as to what is best to be done.

Aaron Burr

10. To do anything in this world worth doing, you must not stand back shivering and thinking of the cold and danger but jump in and scramble through as well as you can.

Sydney Smith

Activity 3

Understanding Sentence Unscrambling

Practice 1

Choose the meaningful chunking of the sentence.

1. When his father / who was old / and twisted with toil / made over to / him the ownership of the / farm and seemed / content to creep away to / a corner and wait for / death, he / shrugged his shoulders and dismissed the old / man from his mind.

2. When his father / who was old / and twisted with toil / made over to him the ownership / of the farm / and seemed content / to creep away / to a corner / and wait for death / he shrugged his shoulders / and dismissed the old man / from his mind.

   Sherwood Anderson, Winesburg, Ohio

Unscrambling professionally written sentences helps you to understand how effective writers arrange their sentence parts. Study these two lists of sentence parts: first, the original order of sentence parts; next, the scrambled order.

Original Order	**Scrambled Order**
1. When his father,	1. to a corner
2. who was old	2. from his mind.
3. and twisted with toil,	3. and wait for death,
4. made over to him the ownership	4. When his father,
5. of the farm	5. he shrugged his shoulders
6. and seemed content	6. made over to him the ownership
7. to creep away	7. who was old
8. to a corner	8. and dismissed the old man

9. and wait for death,

10. he shrugged his shoulders

11. and dismissed the old man

12. from his mind.

9. of the farm

10. and twisted with toil,

11. to creep away

12. and seemed content

Practice 2

Beneath the model sentence are two lists of scrambled nonsense sentence parts. Unscramble and write out each list to produce sentences with sentence parts arranged and punctuated like the model.

> Model: When his father, who was old and twisted with toil, made over to him the ownership of the farm and seemed content to creep away to a corner and wait for death, he shrugged his shoulders and dismissed the old man from his mind.
> *Sherwood Anderson,* Winesburg, Ohio

List One: Nonsense Sentence Parts (in scrambled order)

1. and covered the floor

2. and feathered with grease

3. with its pizzas

4. which was solid

5. when the ashtray

6. sang for him the dance

7. and became encouraged

8. to an ocean

9. the crab blanked its pencil

10. and hope for mud

11. of the petunia

12. to jump up

List Two: Nonsense Sentence Parts (in scrambled order)

1. in an instant

2. which was crystal

3. the bun opened its halves

4. although the hamburger

5. ran down to him the story

6. in a dictionary

7. of the onion

8. and demented in town

9. and seemed reluctant

10. and study for words

11. to fly away

12. and embraced the cheese

Match and then list the twelve sentence parts in all three sentences—the model and its two imitations. Here is an example for the first sentence part:

Example

From the model: When his father, ...

From scrambled list one: When the ashtray, ...

From scrambled list two: Although the hamburger, ...

---

*A*ctivity 4

Unscrambling Sentence Parts

Practice 1

Sentence parts can often be put in various places within a sentence. Unscramble each sentence three times, and tell which versions are effective and which aren't.

Example

Scrambled Sentence Parts

a. when looking out of her window

b. was a hearse

c. the first thing she saw

Unscrambled Sentences (Three Versions)

1. The first thing she saw when looking out of her window was a hearse.

2. The first thing she saw was a hearse when looking out of her window.

3. When looking out of her window, the first thing she saw was a hearse.

The first version is the original by Gaston Leroux in his novel *The Phantom of the Opera*. The third version is equally effective. The second version is ineffective because the order of information is wrong: The reader needs to know that she was looking out a window before being told what she saw.

1a. the boy's father sat

b. the lantern still burning by his side.

c. at the foot of one of the trees

William H. Armstrong, Sounder

2a. a mortgage financier

b. the father was respectable and tight

c. and forecloser

d. and a stern, upright collection-plate passer
    From a sentence by O. Henry, "The Ransom of Red Chief"

3a. for nothing can be done

b. after Buck Fanshaw's inquest

c. without a public meeting

d. a meeting of the short-haired brotherhood was held

e. on the Pacific coast

f. and an expression of sentiment
    From a sentence by Mark Twain, "Buck Fanshaw's Funeral"

4a. the littlest

b. with them

c. I had ever seen

d. carrying a gnarled walking stick

e. oldest man

f. was Elmo Goodhue Pipgrass
    From a sentence by Max Shulman, "The Unlucky Winner"

5a. over long woolen underwear

b. he bounded

c. around his chest

d. out of bed

e. and a leather jacket

f. wearing a long flannel nightgown

g. a nightcap
From a sentence by James Thurber, "The Night the Ghost Got In"

6a. looked up from his scrambled eggs

  b. once upon a sunny morning

  c. who sat in a breakfast nook

  d. quietly cropping the roses

  e. with a gold horn

  f. a man

  g. to see a white unicorn

  h. in the garden

From a sentence by James Thurber, "The Unicorn in the Garden"

7a. grabbed my right foot

  b. of patent-leather dancing pumps

  c. then

  d. and shoved it into one of them

  e. as a shoehorn

  f. she removed the gleaming pair

  g. out of a box on the bed

  h. using her finger

Jean Shepherd, "Wanda Hickey's Night of Golden Memories"

8a. such as weather balloons

  b. as a general rule

  c. satellites

  d. of the World Trade Center

  e. careful on-the-scene investigations disclose

  f. meteorites

  g. that most "unidentified" flying objects are quite ordinary phenomena

  h. who blew off the roof

    i. named Lewis Mandelbaum

    j. and even once a man

Woody Allen, "The UFO Menace"

9a. had been stowed

  b. in which

  c. the barnyard sounds

  d. escaped from two crates

  e. that we heard

  f. and from a burlap bag

  g. of hens

  h. a small flock

  i. that the Duvitches had fetched along

  j. of ducks

Ambrose Flack, "The Strangers That Came to Town"

10a. in his trouser band

  b. of age

  c. I was fourteen years

  d. that he carried

  e. when a coward

  f. plus two California gold pieces

  g. shot my father down

  h. going by the name of Tom Chaney

  i. and robbed him of his life

  j. in Fort Smith, Arkansas,

  k. and his horse and $150 in cash money

Charles Portis, True Grit

Practice 2

The sentences below have movable sentence parts that are underlined. Reposition the sentence parts. Make sure that your sentence is as effective as the original.

Example

Original Sentence:

Tom was on his feet, <u>shouting</u>.
> *Hal Borland,* When the Legends Die

Effective Rearrangements:

<u>Shouting</u>, Tom was on his feet.

Tom, <u>shouting</u>, was on his feet.

---

1. Taran cried, <u>his teeth chattering violently</u>.
   > *Lloyd Alexander,* The Book of Three

2. The fog horn was blowing steadily, <u>once every fifteen seconds</u>.
   > *Ray Bradbury,* "The Fog Horn"

3. He sat on a rail fence, <u>watching the night come over Gettysburg</u>.
   > *Michael Shaara,* The Killer Angels

4. Slowly, <u>filled with dissatisfaction</u>, he had gone to his room and got into bed.
   > *Betsy Byars,* The Summer of the Swans

5. There are boys from broken homes, and boys who have been in difficulty with the law, <u>studying in the classrooms, working in the fields and in the workshops</u>.
   > *William E. Barrett,* The Lilies of the Field

6. Somewhere there, on that desolate plain, was lurking this fiendish man, hiding in a burrow like a wild beast, <u>his heart full of malignancy against the whole race which had cast him out</u>.
   > *Sir Arthur Conan Doyle,* The Hound of the Baskervilles

7. Alan made a business of checking his own reflection in the mirror, <u>giving Norris time to make a clean getaway</u>, while Keeton stood by the door, <u>watching him impatiently</u>.

    Stephen King, Needful Things

8. Standing in front of the room, <u>her blond hair pulled back to emphasize the determination of her face</u>, <u>her body girdled to emphasize the determination of her spine</u>, <u>her eyes holding determinedly to anger</u>, Miss Lass was afraid.

    Rosa Guy, The Friends

9. She ate a great deal and afterward fell asleep herself, and Mary sat and stared at her and watched her fine bonnet slip on one side until she herself fell asleep once more in the corner of the carriage, <u>lulled by the splashing of the rain against the windows</u>.

    Frances Hodgson Burnett, The Secret Garden

10. The garden was <u>to the left of the barn and the pasture</u> hidden from the house by the smokehouse and a pecan grove and a row of little peach trees that <u>because of the drought</u> had dropped hard knotty fruit not even fit to make spiced pickle with.

    Olive Ann Burns, Cold Sassy Tree

*A*ctivity 5

Unscrambling Paragraphs

Practice 1

Each list below, when unscrambled, will become one of the sentences in a paragraph from Michael Crichton's *Jurassic Park*. In that paragraph, a tyrannosaur attacks a Land Cruiser (car) containing two children, a brother and sister, during a thunderstorm. Unscramble the lists to produce the four sentences in the paragraph. In each list, the part that begins the sentence is capitalized.

1a. with a muddy splash

  b. The rear of the car

  c. and then it thumped down

  d. into the air for a moment

  e. lifted up

2a. of the car

  b. Then it moved

  c. around the side

3a. that blended with the thunder

  b. At the back

  c. a deep rumbling growl

  d. the animal snorted,

4a. out of all the side windows

  b. The big raised tail

  c. blocked their view

5a. mounted on the back of the Land Cruiser

  b. and,

c. It sank its jaws into the spare tire

d. tore it away

e. in a single head shake,

After unscrambling the sentences, arrange the sentences according to this outline:

Sentence One: approach by animal

Sentence Two: car windows blocked

Sentence Three: sounds of animal

Sentence Four: attack to part of car

Sentence Five: lifting of car

Write out and punctuate the paragraph.

Practice 2

Each list below, when unscrambled, will become one of the sentences in a paragraph from Edgar Allan Poe's "The Fall of the House of Usher." In that paragraph, the mysterious main character, Lady Madeline of Usher, is described. Unscramble the lists to produce the four sentences in the paragraph. In each list, the sentence part that begins the sentence is capitalized.

1a. there *did* stand the lofty and shrouded figure

  b. but then without those doors

  c. It was the work of the rushing gust—

  d. of the Lady Madeline of Usher

2a. and the evidence of some bitter struggle

  b. There was blood

  c. upon every portion of her emaciated frame

   d. upon her white robes,

3a. there had been found the potency of a spell,

   b. upon the instant, their ponderous and ebony jaws

   c. As if in the superhuman energy of his utterance

   d. the huge antique panels

   e. to which the speaker pointed

   f. threw slowly back,

4a. to and fro upon the threshold—

   b. bore him to the floor a corpse,

   c. upon the person of her brother,

   d. he had anticipated

   e. then, with a low, moaning cry,

   f. and in her violent and now final death-agonies,

   g. For a moment she remained trembling and reeling

   h. fell heavily inward

   i. and a victim to the terrors

After unscrambling the sentences, arrange the sentences according to this outline:

Sentence One: setting the stage

Sentence Two: introduction of Lady Madeline

Sentence Three: description of Lady Madeline

Sentence Four: action of Lady Madeline

Write out and punctuate the paragraph.

*A*ctivity 6

Avoiding Comma Splices

The most common punctuation error in student writing is when two sentences are joined (spliced) together with only a comma between them. This error, called a comma splice (or run-on sentence), creates problems because readers can't tell where one sentence ends and the next begins.

In all of the following practices in this text, avoid writing comma splices. To help you learn how to eliminate them, do activities 6 and 7.

Example of a Comma Splice

His heart pounding, his lungs inhaling and exhaling like a bellows, Alfred, lunging toward his opponent Jacobs in the third round with his left, swung but missed ⊙ recovering from the miss, he turned swiftly, aimed again, and this time connected squarely with Jacobs' jaw.

Robert Lipsyte, The Contender

Use one of these four ways to eliminate comma splices:

1. Make two sentences:
   His heart pounding, his lungs inhaling and exhaling like a bellows, Alfred, lunging toward his opponent Jacobs in the third round with his left, swung but missed. *Recovering* from the miss, he turned swiftly, aimed again, and this time connected squarely with Jacobs' jaw.

2. Keep the comma but add *and, but, or, so, yet,* or *for* (coordinating conjunctions) to join the sentences:
   His heart pounding, his lungs inhaling and exhaling like a bellows, Alfred, lunging toward his opponent Jacobs in the third round with his left, swung but missed, *but* recovering from the miss, he turned swiftly, aimed again, and this time connected squarely with Jacobs' jaw.

3. Change the comma to a semicolon:
   His heart pounding, his lungs inhaling and exhaling like a bellows, Alfred, lunging toward his opponent Jacobs in the

third round with his left, swung but missed ☉ recovering from the miss, he turned swiftly, aimed again, and this time connected squarely with Jacobs' jaw.

4. Change the comma to a semicolon, and add *nevertheless, however, therefore, moreover, in fact, for example, consequently*, or *as a result* (conjunctive adverbs), and put a comma after the conjunctive adverb:
His heart pounding, his lungs inhaling and exhaling like a bellows, Alfred, lunging toward his opponent Jacobs in the third round with his left, swung but missed ☉ *however*, recovering from the miss, he turned swiftly, aimed again, and this time connected squarely with Jacobs' jaw.

Practice 1

Locate and eliminate the comma splice by making that comma a period and capitalizing the next word to create two separate sentences.

1a. When Mark Twain,

  b. the famous author

  c. whose real name was Samuel Clemens,

  d. was a boy of fourteen,

  e. he thought his father was stupid,

  f. when Twain reached 21,

  g. he was amazed how much his father had learned.

2a. Extremely arrogant and conceited

  b. Jackson didn't understand how his overpowering style affected his lack of friends,

  c. his manager,

  d. after watching his ego swell after the game,

  e. told him to think more of others, and less of himself.

3a. Oatmeal,

b. that common breakfast cereal,

c. is not just for breakfast anymore,

d. mushy and semidisgusting,

e. it's good for other things,

f. like putting in your little brother's shoes,

g. his baseball glove,

h. or his ears.

4a. As the storm,

b. a blizzard that lasted two days,

c. covered the landscape,

d. blanketing everything in white,

e. Jake Slatterly,

f. whose job was to make sure provisions were ample,

g. began to worry,

h. he made a plan,

i. one that was by no means certain of success,

j. to hitch one of the horses to a wagon,

k. drive the little-used road on the other side of the mountain,

l. and with luck and a lot of prayers,

m. get to town to buy some grub and coffee.

Practice 2

Locate and eliminate the comma that is the comma splice, using a variety of ways to eliminate the comma splice. (Review pp. 18–19.)

1. In large metropolitan areas, the yellow pages are a useful means of locating businesses, services, and products, the average customer would be lost without this aid.

2. Very overweight and stocky, Mr. Jackson didn't understand fully how his weight problem affected his health, his doctor, after giving him a physical, put him on a strict diet of fruits, vegetables, and lean meat.

3. I am not ashamed to admit it, I do enjoy reading a good book, one which is entertaining, one which stimulates my thinking, and one which captures my imagination.

4. Sliding over the ice-covered road, the car lost traction briefly, spun toward the edge of the highway, but finally righted itself, the car in the other lane, fortunately, moved out of the way.

5. Wandering aimlessly for days, Indiana Jones couldn't escape the dreaded banana bearers, his companion, after surveying the situation, suggested they put bags over their heads, run around in circles, and climb trees quickly.

*A*ctivity 7

Identifying and Removing Comma Splices

Practice 1

Below is a description of a football player nicknamed Darling making a long run for a touchdown from Irwin Shaw's "The Eighty-Yard Run." In each list, one of the commas is a comma splice that was not in the original. Remove each comma splice using one of the four ways to eliminate comma splices.

In doing this practice, you will see that comma splices create problems for readers, and must be eliminated.

1a. The pass was high and wide,

  b. and Darling jumped for it,

  c. feeling it slap flatly against his hands as he shook his hips to throw off the halfback who was diving at him,

  d. the center floated by,

  e. his hands desperately brushing Darling's knee as Darling picked his feet up high and delicately ran over a blocker and an opposing linesman in a jumble on the ground near the scrimmage line.

2a. He smiled a little to himself as he ran,

  b. holding the ball lightly in front of him,

  c. his knees pumping high,

  d. his hips twisting in the almost girlish run of a back in a broken field,

  e. the first halfback came at him,

  f. and Darling fed him his leg,

  g. then swung at the last moment,

  h. took the shock of the man's shoulder without breaking stride,

    i. ran right through him,

    j. his cleats biting securely into the turf.

3a. There was only the safety man now,

    b. coming warily at him,

    c. his arms crooked,

    d. hands spread,

    e. he tucked the ball in,

    f. spurted at him,

    g. driving hard,

    h. hurling himself along,

    i. his legs pounding,

    j. knees high,

    k. all two hundred pounds bunched into controlled attack.

4a. Without thought,

    b. his arms and legs working beautifully together,

    c. Darling headed right for the safety man,

    d. stiff-armed him,

    e. feeling blood spurt instantaneously from the man's nose onto his hand,

    f. seeing his face go awry,

    g. head turned,

    h. mouth pulled to one side,

    i. Darling pivoted away,

    j. keeping the arm locked,

    k. dropping the safety man as he ran easily toward the goal line,

    l. with the drumming of cleats diminishing behind him.

Practice 2

Five of the twenty-one commas below are comma splices that were not in the original paragraphs. Tell the numbers of the comma splices, copy the paragraphs, and then eliminate comma splices using whatever way seems effective. (To review the four ways to eliminate comma splices, see Activity 6.)

The May sunset was red in clouds (1), and there was still half an hour to twilight (2), the dry slope was dotted with rabbits (3), some nibbling at the thin grass near their holes (4), others pushing further down to look for dandelions or perhaps a cowslip that the rest had missed. Here and there one sat upright on an ant heap and looked about (5), with ears erect and nose in the wind (6), a blackbird (7), singing undisturbed on the outskirts of the wood (8), showed that there was nothing alarming there (9), and in the other direction (10), along the brook (11), all was plain to be seen (12), empty and quiet (13), the warren was at peace.

At the top of the bank (14), close to the wild cherry where the blackbird sang (15), was a little group of holes almost hidden by brambles (16), in the green half-light (17), at the mouth of one of these holes (18), two rabbits were sitting together side by side. At length (19), the larger of the two came out (20), slipped along the bank under cover of the brambles and so down into the ditch and up into the field (21), a few moments later the other followed.

Richard Adams, Watership Down

Activity 8

Varying Sentence Structure

Practice 1

In the paragraphs below, practice sentence variety by moving sentence parts to new places. Move the underlined sentence parts to places equally effective. Write out the new paragraphs.

1. As quickly as it had come, the wind died, and the clearing was quiet again. The heron stood in the shallows, motionless and waiting. A little water snake swam up the pool, turning its periscope head from side to side.

    John Steinbeck, Of Mice and Men

2. Behind us was the town of Castle Rock, spread out on the long hill that was known as Castle View, surrounding its green and shady common. Further down Castle River you could see the stacks of the woolen mill spewing smoke into a sky the color of gunmetal and spewing waste into the water. The Jolly Furniture Barn was on our left, and straight ahead of us were the railroad tracks, bright and heliographing in the sun.

    Stephen King, "The Body"

3. Standing at the front window and holding back the curtain, Agatha watched for the first star. In the summertime she had to be alert because the sky stayed light for so long that the stars would more or less melt into view. Sometimes Thomas waited, too. He said his wishes aloud, no matter how often she warned him not to. He wished for definite objects—toys and candy and such—as if the sky were one big Sears, Roebuck catalog. Agatha, on the other hand, wished silently, and not even in words. She wished in a strong wash of feeling.

    Anne Tyler, Saint Maybe

4. We paid our dollars at the admission gate and threw ourselves into the carnival like famished beggars at a feast.

The strings of light bulbs gleamed <u>over our heads like trapped stars</u>. A lot of kids our age were there, <u>along with their parents</u>, and some older people and high school kids, too. <u>Around us</u> the rides grunted, clattered, and rattled. We bought our tickets and got on the Ferris wheel, and I made the mistake of sitting with Davy Ray. <u>When we got to the very top and the wheel paused to allow riders on the bottom-most gondola</u>, he grinned and started rocking us back and forth and yelling that the bolts were about to come loose.

Robert R. McCammon, Boy's Life

Practice 2

From your own writing, choose several paragraphs to practice sentence variety by re-positioning the parts in your sentences. Identify the parts of the sentences that can be re-positioned, and then rewrite those sentences, moving those parts to new places.

2

Sentence Imitating

In this part of the worktext, you will learn how to imitate sentences written by professional writers. You will learn and practice how those writers vary their sentences. As you imitate their sentences, pay attention to how they composed them. Apply what you learn to your own sentences.

*A*ctivity 9

Matching Sentence Structures

Practice 1

Unscramble and write out each list to make a sentence that imitates the model.

Example

Model: He turned, his back to the distant fire, and peered into the dark.

Anne Rice, Interview with the Vampire

Scrambled Sentence Parts

a. her fingers drumming on the table

b. she waited

c. and then paced around the room

Unscrambled Imitation of Model

She waited, her fingers drumming on the table, and then paced around the room.

---

1. Model: The bear dropped to all fours, whimpering.

    Hal Borland, When the Legends Die

    a. running

    b. in all directions

    c. the class scattered

2. Model: As time went on, I began to depend more and more on my left foot for everything.

    Christy Brown, My Left Foot

    a. in the stadium

    b. louder and louder

c. the crowd started to shout

d. when the winner appeared

3. Model: Dazed, suffering intolerable pain from throat and tongue, with the life half throttled out of him, Buck attempted to face his tormentors.

Jack London, The Call of the Wild

a. because of vacation

b. refreshed

c. in a mood

d. from pressure and performance

e. he started to swing his tennis racket

f. much improved

g. feeling tremendous relief

4. Model: He felt a heavy, sighing peace, like a soldier who has been comfortably wounded and knows that war for him is over.

Edmund Ware, "An Underground Episode"

a. now must be guarded

b. of honesty

c. who has often been hurt

d. he spoke

e. like a friend

f. and believes that expressions

g. one slow, nervous sentence

5. Model: Six boys came over the hill half an hour early that afternoon, running hard, their heads down, their forearms working, their breath whistling.

John Steinbeck, The Red Pony

a. their arms up

b. in the gym

c. their bodies swaying

d. during the last dance that night

e. prom dancers spun around

f. the band blaring

g. stomping loudly

Practice 2

Underneath each model sentence are two scrambled imitations of the model. One makes sense, the other, nonsense. However, when both are unscrambled, both will match the structure of the model. Unscramble and write out each to produce sentences with sentence parts arranged and punctuated like the model.

Model: Tom got his lantern, lit it in the hogshead, wrapped it closely in the towel, and the two adventurers crept in the gloom toward the tavern.

Mark Twain, Tom Sawyer

1a. ahead of the singer

b. rehearsed it

c. Bob wrote his song

d. but the small orchestra played

e. sang it beautifully

f. in the play

g. in the evenings

h. with the beat

2a. and the plimey peesto scrunted

b. broded it

c. in the tunert

d. Snaze kurped its blander

e. crassed it frinkly

f. of a bleepert

g. from the marton

h. with the snart

Model: To carry care to bed is to sleep with a pack on your back.
Thomas Haliburton

3a. in a state

b. to bring work

c. of constant worry

d. is

e. from the office

f. to "relax"

4a. in a zipple

b. to jeld crams

c. is

d. near town

e. from a zapple

f. to murd

Model: The man who writes about himself and his own time is the only man who writes about all people and about all time.
George Bernard Shaw

5a. with great enthusiasm

b. a sportscaster

c. and with solid knowledge

d. the choice announcer

e. is

f. who communicates

g. who communicates

h. and sports' top athletes

i. with fans

6a. and near forty bloops

  b. the blends

  c. the best blends

  d. and their brained nabort

  e. which croak

  f. are

  g. which croak

  h. near thirty bleeps

  i. from selfhoose

Model: A leather handbag, extremely worn, but with a label inside it as impressive as the one inside Mrs. Snell's hat, lay on the pantry.

J.D. Salinger, "Down at the Dinghy"

7a. very dry

  b. in Grandma's eyes

  c. as appealing

  d. the wrinkled skin

  e. as the sparkle

  f. shone in the candlelight

  g. about it

  h. yet with a softness

8a. an oversized saltert

  b. in its woostem

  c. quite pritert

  d. as lumrious

  e. plazoned from a yambrod

  f. as a klanion

  g. on it

  h. and of a color

*A*ctivity 10

Identifying Sentence Imitations

Practice 1

Below are pairs of sentences consisting of a model sentence and a student imitation of the model. Copy the sentences and divide them with slash lines into similar sentence parts.

Example

Model: One of the pups / came slowly toward me, / a round ball of fur / that I could have held in my hand.
                    Scott O'Dell, Island of the Blue Dolphins

Student Imitation: The principal of the school / jogged in the halls, / an advocate for fitness / who inspired students and faculty.

1a. Model: Suddenly, Archie felt empty, used up, discarded.
                    Robert Cormier, The Chocolate War

 b. Imitation: Eventually, the team became better, unified, victorious.

2a. Model: By dawn, the house smelled of Sunday: chicken frying, bacon sizzling, and smoke sausages baking.
                    Mildred D. Taylor, Roll of Thunder, Hear My Cry

 b. Imitation: At the pool, the scene was varied: kids splashing, teens socializing, adults supervising.

3a. Model: Jimbo danced all over the place, clapping his paws, squalling, grunting, and turning somersaults.
                    Wilson Rawls, Summer of the Monkeys

 b. Imitation: Jason skated during the finals, doing figure eights, swirling, leaping, and wowing the crowd.

4a. Model: Strolling back under the warm summer elms toward the house, Aunt Rose suddenly gasped and put her hand to her throat.
                    Ray Bradbury, Dandelion Wine

b. Imitation: Lying down in the middle of the living room carpet, the dog turned over on its back and imitated a dead roach.

5a. Model: Frank and George produced a bucket of water and a scrubbing brush and gave me a rough clean-up before I left.
James Herriot, All Creatures Great and Small

b. Imitation: The coach and the team captain shouted final directions and a pep talk and gave each member a handshake before the players ran onto the field.

Practice 2

In each group of three sentences below, chunk each one, and then identify the two sentences with similar sentence parts. In other words, one sentence imitates another.

Example

a. The snow froze / when the temperature dipped / during the night / and the water from the gradual thaw / turned to ice.

b. The principal of the school / jogged in the halls / a believer in fitness / who inspired students and faculty.

c. One of the pups / came slowly toward me / a round ball of fur / that I could have held in my hand.

Answer: b and c (similar sentence parts)

1a. Great was his care of them.

b. Something else he saw.

c. Chilling was her story of passion.

2a. The big thing, exciting yet frightening, was to talk to her, say what he hoped to do.

b. There was also a rhino, who, from the tracks and the kicked-up mound of strawy dung, came there each night.

c. An acceptable solution, simple and efficient, is to negotiate with the management, emphasize what the workers want to delete.

3a. Much later the accountant finished, ledgers in their vertical files on the right side of the desk, pencils and pens in the container decorated with seals and designs on the shelf above the desk.

b. This leader, whose word was law among boys who defied authority for the sake of defiance, was no more than twelve or thirteen years old and looked even younger.

c. Soon afterward they retired, Mama in her big oak bed on one side of the room, Emilio and Rosy in their boxes full of straw and sheepskins on the other side of the room.

4a. During rush-hour traffic, when his nerves were frazzled, Brent Hammond, twenty miles above the speed limit, hit his brakes, from which came sharp peals and leaden grindings as though the metal were alive and hurting.

b. On stormy nights, when the tide was out, the bay of Fougere, fifty feet below the house, resembled an immense black pit, from which arose mutterings and sighs as if the sands down there had been alive and complaining.

c. Aleck Sander stood out from the shadows, walking, already quite near in the moonless dark, a little taller than Big Ed, though there was only a few months' difference between them.

*A*ctivity 11

Identifying Models and Imitations

Practice 1

Each of the four model sentences below has two imitations. Identify the imitations for each model.

Model Sentences

1. Near the spot upriver to which Mr. Tanimoto had transported the priests, there sat a large case of rice cakes which a rescue party had evidently brought for the wounded lying thereabouts but hadn't distributed.

   John Hersey, Hiroshima

2. There was also a rhino, who, from the tracks and the kicked-up mound of strawy dung, came there each night.

   Ernest Hemingway, Green Hills of Africa

3. The dark silence was there and the heavy shapes, sitting, and the little blue light burning.

   Ray Bradbury, The Vintage Bradbury

4. Light flickered on bits of ruby glass and on sensitive capillary hairs in the nylon-brushed nostrils of the creature that quivered gently, gently, its eight legs spidered under it on rubber-padded paws.

   Ray Bradbury, Fahrenheit 451

Imitations

a. Stars twinkled on pieces of broken shells and on ruined sand castles in the sea-drenched sand of the beach that stretched miles, endless miles, its many shells strewn on it by high-crested waves.

b. At the place in the room where he had left his books, there was a stack of journals that had evidently been brought by several of the more academic students but hadn't been used by the teacher.

c. The dense fog was there and the bloody bodies, dying, and the torn white flag waving.

d. I sat on velvet grass and under spreading blue leaves in the light-yellow atmosphere of a planet that orbited, slowly, steadily, its six moons clinging close like new-born children.

e. There was also a turtle, who, from the half-eaten tomato and the hole under the fence, had visited the garden that day.

f. The big race was ready to begin and the line of cars, waiting, and the red flag still standing.

g. There was also the horror, which, from the odor and snake-belly sensation of dead flesh, came there each time.

h. Outside the shack from which the patrol had started shooting, there was a blast of gunfire that the rebels had intended for the door lock but hadn't hit.

Practice 2

Write an imitation of each of the four model sentences in Practice 1.

Activity 12

Learning How to Imitate Sentences

Practice 1

In this practice you will learn how to analyze all the sentence parts of a model sentence and then imitate the model sentence by writing similar sentence parts. Below is a four-sentence paragraph from *A Wrinkle in Time* by Madeleine L'Engle. Underneath each model is a scrambled sentence imitation. Unscramble the sentence parts to match the model, and write out the complete sentence, correctly punctuated.

1. Model: Calvin and Meg walked carefully / across the vegetable garden, / picking their way through rows / of cabbages, beets, broccoli, and pumpkins.

   Scrambled Imitation:

   a. of books, notebooks, loose pages, pens, and pencils

   b. sorting through the heap on the floor

   c. in the hallway

   d. Levon and James stood together

2. Model: Looming on their left / were the tall stalks of corn.

   Scrambled Imitation:

   a. was the menacing shadow of their homeroom teacher

   b. appearing in a nearby doorway

3. Model: Ahead of them / was a small apple orchard / bounded by a stone wall, / and beyond this the woods / which they had walked that afternoon.

   Scrambled Imitation:

   a. and scattered there the debris

   b. on the floor below them

   c. was Levon's bookbag

   d. that he had dropped just seconds before

   e. strewn open from the fall

4. Model: Calvin led the way to the wall, / and then sat there, / his red hair / shining silver in the moonlight, / his body / dappled with patterns from the tangle of branches.

   Scrambled Imitation:

   a. and then knelt there

   b. his face

   c. Levon bent his body toward the floor

   d. his hands

   e. hidden from the stare of his teacher in the doorway

   f.   vacuuming the contents into the bookbag

Practice 2

Imitate the four sentences from the paragraph from *A Wrinkle in Time*, using the sentence parts of the model, which are indicated by slash marks in the model and sample student imitation.

1. Model: Calvin and Meg walked carefully / across the vegetable garden, / picking their way through rows / of cabbages, beets, broccoli, pumpkins.

   Student Imitation: Happy-Dog and Rover played together / in the backyard, / chasing each other / along the fenceline, bushes, trees, trash cans.

2. Model: Looming on their left / were the tall stalks of corn.

   Student Imitation: Standing on the back porch / were the owners of the two dogs.

3. Model: Ahead of them / was a small apple orchard / bounded by a stone wall, / and beyond this the woods / which they had walked that afternoon.

Student Imitation: In the yard's corner / was the neighbor's cat / huddled into a fur ball, / and next to the cat the neighbor / who was watching all the rumpus.

4. Model: Calvin led the way to the wall, / and then sat there, / his red hair / shining silver in the moonlight, / his body / dappled with patterns from the tangle of branches.

Student Imitation: The dogs romped their way toward the corner, / and suddenly stopped, / their ears / standing upright in a frozen position, / their faces / bemused with surprise from the sudden appearance of the cat.

Activity 13

Imitating Sentence Variety (Part One)

Practice 1

Imitate these new model sentences, using your own content but the same structure as sentence parts in the model. Imitate one sentence part at a time. Aim for approximating, not duplicating, the model. If your imitations somewhat resemble the models, they are successful.

Example

Model: Mollie, the foolish, pretty white mare who drew Mr. Jones's trap, came mincing daintily in, chewing at a lump of sugar.

George Orwell, Animal Farm

Sample Student Imitation: The garbage disposal, a noisy, chewing metal mouth that ate the meal's leftovers, began gurgling suddenly then, spitting up a half-eaten carrot.

---

1. Model: Great was his care of them.

   Jack London, All Gold Canyon

   Sample Student Imitation: Chilling was her story of anger.

2. Model: The big thing, exciting yet frightening, was to talk to her, say what he hoped to do.

   Bernard Malamud, The Assistant

   Sample Student Imitation: An acceptable solution, simple and obvious, is to talk with the manager, emphasize what the workers want to request.

3. Model: He had never been hungrier, and he filled his mouth with wine, faintly tarry-tasting from the leather bag, and swallowed.

   Ernest Hemingway, For Whom the Bell Tolls

Sample Student Imitation: The horse had never been nastier, and it threw its riders to the ground, cold and hard from the frost, and bolted.

4. Model: Soon afterwards they retired, Mama in her big oak bed on one side of the room, Emilio and Rosy in their boxes full of straw and sheepskins on the other side of the room.

John Steinbeck, Flight

Sample Student Imitation: Much later the accountant finished, computer disks in their neat boxes on the right side of the desk, pencils and pens in their containers decorated with seals and designs on the shelf above the desk.

5. Model: On stormy nights, when the tide was out, the bay of Fougere, fifty feet below the house, resembled an immense black pit, from which arose mutterings and sighs as if the sands down there had been alive and complaining.

Joseph Conrad, "The Idiots"

Sample Student Imitation: During rush-hour traffic, when his nerves were frazzled, Brent Hammond, a few miles above the speed limit, hit his brakes, from which came sharp peals and leaden grindings as though the metal were alive and hurting.

Practice 2

Write a paragraph describing an object or telling a story. Somewhere in the paragraph include imitations of *two* of the model sentences below, one from the list of short models, and one from the list of long models. Try to make all sentences, not just the imitations, effective and varied like sentences of professional writers. If you succeed, your imitations will be *invisible* because your own sentences will be as good as the two you wrote imitating model sentences.

Short Model Sentences (Choose and imitate *one* to include in your paragraph.)

1. Jethro squirmed inwardly.

Irene Hunt, Across Five Aprils

2. Meg began to cry, to sob aloud.
   Madeleine L'Engle, A Wrinkle in Time

3. As darkness closed in, the rain stopped.
   Richard Adams, Watership Down

4. His own shadow reappeared, dark and long and clearcut.
   Stephen King, "Secret Window, Secret Garden"

5. Shortly after Yvonne was born came the nightmare night in
   1929, my earliest vivid memory.
   Malcolm X, The Autobiography of Malcolm X

**Long Model Sentences (Choose and imitate *one* to include in
your paragraph.)**

1. The first gray light had just appeared in the living room
   windows, black mirrors a moment ago, now opening on the
   view of the woods to the south.
   Tracy Kidder, Old Friends

2. When I peeped into the sickroom again, Grandpa was bent
   forward in the rocker, his arms and head resting on the bed
   by Granny's side.
   Olive Ann Burns, Cold Sassy Tree

3. She was no more than twelve, slender, dirty, nervous and
   timid as a bird, but beneath the grime as eerily beautiful as a
   marsh fairy.
   Paul Gallico, The Snow Goose

4. In the dining hall, over the stone fireplace that was never
   used, there was a huge stuffed moose head, which looked
   somehow carnivorous.
   Margaret Atwood, "Death by Landscape"

5. As a girl of ten, Maria had been given a crippled pony, not a
   true pony, but a small, spotted horse that had injured itself
   badly on some barbed wire strung by the men who owned
   the big ranch across the river.
   Larry McMurtry, Streets of Laredo

*A*ctivity 14

Imitating Sentence Variety (Part Two)

Practice 1

Write an imitation of each model sentence.

1. One of these dogs, the best one, had disappeared
   Fred Gibson, Old Yeller

2. Among the company was a lawyer, a young man of about twenty-five.
   Anton Chekhov, "The Bet"

3. Halfway there he heard the sound he dreaded, the hollow, rasping cough of a horse.
   John Steinbeck, The Red Pony

4. Poppa, a good quiet man, spent the last hours before our parting moving aimlessly about the yard, keeping to himself and avoiding me.
   Gordon Parks, "My Mother's Dream for Me"

5. They themselves were a rough lot, dressed in rags, their hats marbled with grease and sweat, their boots mended with raw cowhide.
   Cormac McCarthy, All the Pretty Horses

Practice 2

Write an original paragraph of ten sentences. Include somewhere in your paragraph *two imitations* of any two model sentences below. In the rest of your paragraph, try to write sentences *without the use of models* that are as mature and varied as the model sentences.

Model Sentences

1. The frozen earth thawed, leaving the short grass looking wet and weary.
   Pete Abraham, Tell Freedom

2. Several turtles lay on their backs, flapping their flippers like babies wanting to be changed.

   David Bowman, Let the Dog Drive

3. Over this rocky area relieved by a few shady tall persimmon trees the graduating class walked.

   Maya Angelou, I Know Why the Caged Bird Sings

4. Holding the ladder tightly against his side, he moved toward a spot just beyond the library window.

   James Patterson, Along Came a Spider

5. Strategically placed around the room, most probably by an interior decorator, were bleached oak tables with granite tops, chairs and a sofa in pastel shades and macrame wall hangings.

   Phillip Margolin, Gone But Not Forgotten

6. One minute it was winter, with doors closed, windows locked, the panes blind with frost, icicles fringing every roof, children skiing on slopes, housewives lumbering like great black bears in their coats along the icy streets.

   Ray Bradbury, The Martian Chronicles

*A*ctivity 15

Imitating Sentences in Paragraphs

Practice 1

All of the paragraphs below were written by students who imitated the sentence structures in a professionally written paragraph. The paragraphs are similar, not in content but in sentence structure. Read the paragraphs to identify similarities in sentence structure.

1. When an accident occurs, the car becomes disabled as do the passengers in it. Wear seat belts. Trust that they will work to prevent injury. Know that wearing seat belts will result in less injury, greater survivability, and less prolonged injury.

2. When you start smoking cigarettes, within a few months your body becomes physically addicted. Try not to start. Think ahead about all of the damage it causes the body. Know that when you start smoking eventually you will start coughing, your teeth will turn yellow, and it will be very difficult to quit.

3. When a strong earthquake happens, the earth's surface begins a process as terrible as the anger of a god. Cut off all electrical sources. Get out of your house. Know that the earthquake will end, and when it ends, you will probably survive and be able to recover.

4. When the clouds are full in the sky, the day appears as sad and as dull as wilted flowers. Do not allow this gloom to overpower your spirit. Make the most of this deathly day. Believe that this day will soon be gone, and when it is, you will feel a rebirth of life, strength, and energy.

5. When a baby is born, the body goes through a tremendous change. Let the change occur. It is the natural process of birth. Know that the baby will be born, and when it is born,

you will have a beautiful, healthy baby, more wonderful than you can imagine.

6. When you learn something new, a process as natural as breathing takes place. Become fearful of making mistakes. Don't let that fear stop progress. Know that the knowledge will be mastered, and when it is mastered, you will be more confident, and more willing to try new things.

7. When you begin an exercise program, you should select exercises that are right for you. Try not to duplicate someone else's program. Avoid over training. Begin slowly and eventually increase the frequency and intensity of each workout, and when you do, this will ensure that you do not injure your body.

8. When you begin to eat a lot of fatty foods, in a few months your body will show it. Try not to eat fatty foods. Think about other foods that you can eat that won't make you fat. Know that when you start to eat well, you will live longer, have more energy, and feel better about yourself.

Practice 2

Write your own paragraph that imitates the sentence structures of the paragraphs in Practice 1.

Activity 16

Imitating Long Sentences

Practice 1

The model sentence below, based on a sentence by Martin Luther King, Jr. from "Letter from Birmingham Jail," is a series of similar sentence parts beginning with *when*. Read the sentence several times to analyze the sentence parts.

Model Sentence

When you have seen vicious mobs lynch your mothers and fathers and drown your sisters and brothers, *when* you have seen hate-filled policemen curse and kick your black brothers and sisters, *when* you see the vast majority of your twenty million Negro brothers smothering in an airtight cage of poverty in the midst of a wealthy society, *when* you suddenly find your tongue twisted and your speech stammering as you seek to explain to your six-year-old daughter why she can't go to the public amusement park that has just been advertised on television and see her cry when she is told that Funtown is closed to colored children, *when* you take a long trip and find it necessary to sleep night after night in the uncomfortable corners of your automobile because no motel will accept you, you will then understand the horror of prejudice.

Practice 2

Write an imitation of the model sentence, using, like the model, a series of sentence parts beginning with *when*. For the last sentence part, choose one of these:

1. you will then know what my life is like.

2. you will then get a good idea of what real fun is like.

3. you will then know what real success is.

4. you will then understand why success takes hard work.

5. you will then be aware of what it's like to baby-sit.

6. you will then grasp what it takes to be an athlete.

7. you will then experience real love.

8. you will then know the joy of doing your best.

9. you will then. . . . (Choose one of your own.)

Sentence Parts of Model Sentence

1. *When* you have seen vicious mobs lynch your mothers and fathers and drown your sisters and brothers,

2. *when* you have seen hate-filled policemen curse and kick your black brothers and sisters,

3. *when* you see the vast majority of your twenty million Negro brothers smothering in an airtight cage of poverty in the midst of a wealthy society,

4. *when* you suddenly find your tongue twisted and your speech stammering as you seek to explain to your six-year-old daughter why she can't go to the public amusement park that has just been advertised on television and see her cry when she is told that Funtown is closed to colored children,

5. *when* you take a long trip and find it necessary to sleep night after night in the uncomfortable corners of your automobile because no motel will accept you,

6. you will then understand the horror of prejudice.

Activity 17

Imitating Paragraphs (Part One)

Practice 1

Read the model paragraph and the six paragraphs underneath it. Identify three paragraphs that imitate the sentence structures in the model paragraph.

Model Paragraph

(1) This is a snail shell, round, full, and glossy as a horse chestnut. (2) Comfortable and compact, it sits curled up like a cat in the hollow of my hand. (3) Milky and opaque, it has the pinkish bloom of the sky on a summer evening, ripening to rain. (4) On its smooth, symmetrical face is pencilled with precision a perfect spiral, winding inward to the pinpoint center of the shell, the tiny dark core of the apex, the pupil of the eye. (5) It stares at me, this mysterious single eye—and I stare back.

Paragraph One

(1) The school bus pulled up and let the children out. (2) One of the little boys was running after his dog. (3) The dog had followed him to school and refused to go home when the boy chased him. (4) The other students thought it was funny when the dog ran into the school building. (5) Somebody had left the door open on purpose.

Paragraph Two

(1) When it snowed yesterday, I was at the library. (2) The library is one near where I live and has many books that can help a lot with the assignments from school. (3) A lot of my friends go there to visit with each other and to do some research and studying. (4) The librarians are helpful when you need to find some book to do a history or English assignment. (5) I like the library!

Paragraph Three

(1) There is a snowflake, light, delicate, and fluffy as a piece of cotton. (2) Swirling and blowing, it floats down from the sky like the seeds of the milkweed plant. (3) White and bright, it has the gleam of the blinding sunlight and the reflecting moonlight, shining

in silver. (4) On its surface is stenciled a star, formed with its five or six symmetrical points, the arms of the snowflake, the body of it. (5) It falls to earth, this crystal of beauty—and the earth melts it.

Paragraph Four

(1) This is an old book, interesting, long, but thought-provoking as a philosophical treatise. (2) Soiled but well read, it remains standing upright on my bookshelf mixed in with paperbacks. (3) Analytic and probing, it reveals many pitfalls in the process of thinking, describing wrong conclusions. (4) In its yellow pages are recorded with skill many criticisms, converging ultimately into the story of all people, the universal, timeless tale of every individual, the discourse on humanity. (5) It speaks of man, this lengthy discourse—yet man ignores it.

Paragraph Five

(1) Some rock stars are very colorful and exciting to watch when they perform at a live concert. (2) Usually hundreds or thousands of teenagers attend these concerts, which are usually held in large convention halls or sometimes outdoors in large parks or other public places. (3) Music-lovers look forward to attending these exciting events. (4) Despite what many people say, the behavior at the concerts is very good. (5) It is noisy, but since noise is what anyone would expect at such concerts, nobody there really minds.

Paragraph Six

(1) This is a room, dark, comfortable, and at times lonely as a silent cave. (2) Small and private, it can absorb my thoughts like a sponge. (3) Comfortable and secure, the room has a feeling of safety and peace, providing a hiding place. (4) On its walls are varicolored posters, all reflecting moods of mine, ranging from joy to despair. (5) The posters face me, those mirrors of my soul—and I reminisce.

Practice 2

Write your own imitation of the model paragraph, describing an object or a person—a writing instrument, an old family picture, a pet, a sports player in action, etc. If your prefer, use one of these starter sentences instead:

1. That is an attic, musty, dark, and mysterious as fog.

2. This is a computer, sleek, compact, yet obedient as a highly-trained tiger.

3. Here is a baby, soft, warm, and pink as a rose.

4. That is the new car, shiny, stunning, and responsive as a racehorse.

5. This is a dandelion, feathery, light, and enchanting as fairy dust.

6. This is a marble, sparkling, colorful, and dazzling as a precious stone.

7. Here are the players, uniformed, determined, and coordinated as a well-oiled machine.

8. Those are the paintings, modern, abstract, but brilliant as a Rembrandt.

9. This is a tired eye, glassy, bloodshot, and unfocused as a bad camera shot.

10. That is a rainbow, lovely, shimmering, and elusive as a dream.

Below the sentences are broken down into their sentence parts to help you focus on how each part is written.

1a. This is a snail shell,

b. round, full, and glossy

c. as a horse chestnut.

2a. Comfortable and compact,

b. it sits curled up like a cat

c. in the hollow of my hand.

3a. Milky and opaque,

b. it has the pinkish bloom

c. of the sky on a summer evening,

d. ripening to rain.

4a. On its smooth, symmetrical face

  b. is pencilled with precision a perfect spiral,

  c. winding inward to the pinpoint center of the shell,

  d. the tiny dark core of the apex,

  e. the pupil of the eye.

5a. It stares at me,

  b. this mysterious single eye—

  c. and I stare back.

Activity 18

Imitating Paragraphs (Part Two)

Practice 1

The model paragraph below, from the novel *Of Mice and Men* by John Steinbeck, describes a bunk house where ranch workers live. Read the paragraph to prepare to write an imitation of its sentences in a paragraph of your own.

(1) Inside a long, rectangular building, the bunk house had whitewashed walls and an unpainted floor. (2) In three walls there were small, square windows, and in the fourth, a solid door with a wooden latch. (3) Against the walls were eight bunk beds, five of them made up with blankets, the other three unmade, exposing the burlap ticking on their mattresses. (4) Over each bunk there was nailed a wooden apple crate containing two wooden shelves for the personal possessions of the occupant of the bunk. (5) On these shelves were loaded little articles: soap, shaving cream, combs, brushes, razors, and medicines. (6) Near one wall there was a wood stove, its stovepipe going straight up through the ceiling. (7) In the middle of the room stood a big square table littered with playing cards, and around it were wooden apple boxes for the card players to sit on.

Practice 2

Write your own paragraph describing the interior of some place— your room at home, your classroom, a theater or sports arena, etc. Imitate the sentences in the Steinbeck paragraph, one sentence at a time. Below, those sentences are broken down into their sentence parts to help you focus on how each part is written.

1a. Inside a long, rectangular building,

  b. the bunk house had whitewashed walls

  c. and an unpainted floor.

2a. In three walls there were small, square windows,

b. and in the fourth, a solid door with a wooden latch.

3a. Against the walls were eight bunk beds,

b. five of them made up with blankets,

c. the other three unmade,

d. exposing the burlap ticking on their mattresses.

4a. Over each bunk there was nailed a wooden apple crate

b. containing two wooden shelves

c. for the personal possessions of the occupant of the bunk.

5a. On these shelves were loaded little articles:

b. soap, shaving cream, combs, brushes, razors, and medicines.

Hint: The verb (*were loaded*) comes before, not after the
subject—a reversal of the usual pattern. Also, colons often
introduce lists. Use one to introduce your list of objects, just as
the model sentence does.

6a. Near one wall there was a wood stove,

b. its stovepipe going straight up through the ceiling.

7a. In the middle of the room

b. stood a big square table

c. littered with playing cards,

d. and around it were wooden apple boxes

e. for the card players to sit on.

Activity 19

Imitating an Introductory Paragraph

Practice 1

Below is the first paragraph from *Hiroshima* by John Hersey, a nonfiction account of the survivors of the bombing of Hiroshima during World War II. John Hersey gathered the information through interviewing the survivors. Underneath Hersey's paragraph is a student's imitation, based upon interviews with people who remember what they were doing when they heard that President Kennedy had been assassinated. Read the paragraphs to analyze the similarities in the way the sentences are written.

**MODEL: Opening Paragraph of Hersey's Book
(Bombing of Hiroshima)**

(1) At exactly fifteen minutes past eight in the morning, on August 6, 1945, Japanese time, at the moment when the atomic bomb flashed above Hiroshima, Miss Toshiko Sasaki, a clerk in the personnel department of the East Asia Tin Works, had just sat down at her place in the plant office and was turning her head to speak to the girl at the next desk. (2) At that same moment, Dr. Masakazu Fujii, a well-to-do proprietor of a small hospital, was settling down cross-legged to read the newspaper Asahi on the porch of his private hospital, overhanging one of the seven rivers which divide Hiroshima. (3) Mrs. Hatsuyo Nakamura, a tailor's widow, stood by the window of her kitchen, watching a neighbor tearing down his house because it lay in the path of the air-raid-defense fire lane. (4) Father Wilhelm Kleinsorge, a German priest of the Society of Jesus, reclined in his underwear on a cot on the top floor of his order's three-story mission house, reading a Jesuit magazine. (5) Dr. Terufumi Sasaki, a young member of the surgical staff of the city's large, modern Red Cross Hospital, walked along one of the hospital corridors with a blood specimen for a Wassermann test in his hand. (6) Reverend Tanimoto, the pastor of the Hiroshima Methodist Church, prepared to unload a handcart full of things he had evacuated from town in fear of the massive B-29 raid which everyone expected Hiroshima to suffer. (7) A hundred thousand people were killed by the atomic bomb, and these six were among the survivors.

**IMITATION: Opening Paragraph of a Student's Report
(Assassination of President Kennedy)**

(1) At approximately 1:30 in the afternoon, on November 22, 1963, Baltimore time, at the moment when the world learned of the assassination of President John Fitzgerald Kennedy, Leroy Jackson, a first-year teacher who had recently moved to Baltimore from Pennsylvania, was sorting report cards to prepare for distributing them to his homeroom at a special end-of-the-day homeroom period. (2) At the same time, Trisha Sloan, a senior at Parkville High School who had a crush on JFK, was rehearsing a song in her choir class and was wondering why there was a commotion in the hall. (3) Ken Smithton, a 9th grade student at a private school outside Chicago, was playing Ping-Pong in gym class. (4) Jennifer Constantine, a salesperson at a large department store who had just recently been hired after months of unsuccessfully job searching, was unpacking stock for the shoe department in which she worked. (5) Tanya Rigger, a grandmother of ten grandchildren who often provided day care for her children's children, was baby-sitting some of her grandchildren. (6) Robert Winston, an auto mechanic at a Ford dealership who had just become a first-time father, was working on a tune-up and had a radio playing in his shop. (7) Millions of people were strongly affected by the President's assassination, and these six were among them.

Practice 2

Interview six people about their memories of some event, and then write an imitation of Hersey's paragraph (bombing of Hiroshima) and the sample student paragraph imitating Hersey's (assassination of President Kennedy). Like the model paragraph and sample imitation paragraph, be sure to identify each person with a brief phrase before telling what the person was doing. Choose one of the following events (or one of your own) that the six people you interview are likely to remember:

1. highlights of family members on a recent holiday celebration, birthday, or family gathering

2. activities of friends during the most recent weekend

3. experiences of people watching the last Super Bowl football game on TV

4. memories of people during a recent natural disaster: snowstorm, ice storm, earthquake, tornado, flood, hurricane, etc.

5. recollections of adults of a famous day in history: assassination of a polictical leader, explosion of the Challenger spacecraft, outbreak of war in the Persian Gulf, etc.

After imitating the introductory paragraph, add several more paragraphs explaining in greater detail the activities of the six people during the event. Be sure to use sentence structures that are mature and varied like the ones in your introductory paragraph.

*A*ctivity 20

Imitating Professional Opening Paragraphs

Practice 1

The paragraphs below are the opening paragraphs of famous stories. Think of a story you'd like to write, but just write the opening paragraph of that story. Choose one of the paragraphs below as a model, and imitate the way the sentences are written in that paragraph.

1. He rode into our valley in the summer of '89. I was a kid then, barely topping the backboard of father's old chuck-wagon. I was on the upper rail of our small corral, soaking in the later afternoon sun, when I saw him far down the road where it swung into the valley from the open plain beyond.

   Jack Schaefer, Shane

2. He waited on the stoop until twilight, pretending to watch the sun melt into the dirty gray Harlem sky. Up and down the street transistor radios clicked on and hummed into the sour air. Men dragged out card tables, laughing. Cars cruised through the garbage and broken glass, older guys showing off their Friday night girls.

   Robert Lipsyte, The Contender

3. The driver of the wagon swaying through forest and swamp of the Ohio wilderness was a ragged girl of fourteen. Her mother they had buried near the Monongahela—the girl herself had heaped with torn sods the grave beside the river of the beautiful name. Her father lay shrinking with fever on the floor of the wagon-box, and about him played her brothers and sisters, dirty brats, tattered brats, hilarious brats.

   Sinclair Lewis, Arrowsmith

4. It happened that green and crazy summer when Frankie was twelve years old. This was the summer when for a long time she had not been a member. She belonged to no club and was a member of nothing in the world. Frankie had become

an unjoined person who hung around in doorways, and she was afraid.

Carson McCullers, The Member of the Wedding

5. When Augustus came out on the porch, the pigs were eating a rattlesnake—not a very big one. It had probably just been crawling around looking for shade when it ran into the pigs. They were having a fine tug-of-war with it, and its rattling days were over. The sow had it by the neck, and the shoat had the tail.

Larry McMurtry, Lonesome Dove

6. He rode into the dark of the woods and dismounted. He crawled upward on his belly over cool rocks out into the sunlight, and suddenly he was in the open, and he could see for miles, and there was the whole vast army below him, filling the valley like a smoking river. It came out of a blue rainstorm in the east and overflowed the narrow valley road, coiling along a stream, narrowing and choking a white bridge, fading out into the yellowish dust of June but still visible on the farther road beyond the blue hills, spiked with flags and guidons like a great chopped bristly snake, the snake ending headless in a blue wall of summer rain.

Michael Shaara, The Killer Angels

Practice 2

The sentences below are the opening sentences of famous stories. Choose and copy one of the sentences to begin an opening paragraph of a story. Write the rest of that paragraph. Use mature and varied sentences in your paragraph, similar to the ones you imitated in Practice 1 above. This time, however, create the sentences entirely on your own, without imitating any model sentences.

1. The tall man stood at the edge of the porch.

William H. Armstrong, Sounder

2. First of all, it was October, a rare month for boys.

Ray Bradbury, Something Wicked This Way Comes

3. The drought had lasted now for ten million years, and the reign of the terrible lizards had long since ended.

Arthur C. Clarke, 2001: A Space Odyssey

4. All the beasts in Howling Forest were safe in their caves, nests, and burrows.

Michael Ende, The Neverending Story

5. The Mole had been working very hard all the morning, spring-cleaning his little home.

Kenneth Grahame, The Wind in the Willows

6. Once upon a time there was a Martian named Valentine Michael Smith.

Robert A. Heinlein, Stranger in a Strange Land

7. In the shade of the house, in the sunshine on the river bank by the boats, in the shade of the sallow wood and the fig tree, Siddhartha, the handsome Brahmin's son, grew up with his friend Govinda.

Hermann Hesse, Siddhartha

8. There was once a boy named Milo who didn't know what to do with himself—not just sometimes, but always.

Norton Juster, Phantom Tollbooth

9. The terror, which would not end for another twenty-eight years—if it ever did end—began, so far as I know or can tell, with a boat made from a sheet of newspaper floating down a gutter swollen with rain.

Stephen King, It

10. It was a dark and stormy night.

Madeleine L'Engle, A Wrinkle in Time

11. The island of Gont, a single mountain that lifts its peak a mile above the storm-racked Northeast Sea, is a land famous for wizards.

Ursula K. Le Guin, A Wizard of Earthsea

12. It happened that green and crazy summer when Frankie was twelve years old.

Carson McCullers, The Member of the Wedding

13. On 24 October 1994 planet earth was following its orbit about the sun as it has obediently done for nearly five billion years.

James A. Michener, Space

14. The rattling moving van crept up Brewster like a huge green slug.

Gloria Naylor, The Women of Brewster Place

15. High up on the long hill they called the Saddle Back, behind the ranch and the county road, the boy sat on his horse, facing east, his eyes dazzled by the rising sun.

Mary O'Hara, My Friend Flicka

16. I thought that going to high school was going to be a big improvement over what I was used to.

Daniel Pinkwater, Snarkout Boys and Avocado of Death

17. Miss Polly Harrington entered her kitchen a little hurriedly this June morning.

Eleanor H. Porter, Pollyanna

18. Laurel was thirteen years old.

Olive Higgins Prouty, Stella Dallas

19. A column of smoke rose thin and straight from the cabin chimney.

Marjorie Kinnan Rawlings, The Yearling

20. When Harold was three or four, his father and mother took him to a swimming pool.

John Updike, "Trust Me"

3

Sentence Combining

Sentence combining is a way to express information and ideas in one sentence instead of several. In this section of the worktext you will practice combining pairs and lists of sentences into one sentence to resemble the way professional writers write their sentences.

All of the sentences you will combine are based on sentences written by professional writers. In combining sentences, pay attention to how the writers composed their sentences. Apply what you learn to your own sentences.

*A*ctivity 21

Decombining Sentences

Practice 1

Effective writers can express in one sentence what ineffective writers express in several sentences. To understand the process, take each model sentence and express the content in shorter sentences. Through decombining the model sentences you will see how much more effective the model sentences are compared to the lists of short sentences.

Example

Model: Once his back happened to be half turned toward the door, and, hearing a noise there, he wheeled and sprang up, uttering a loud cry.

Stephen Crane, "The Blue Hotel"

Shorter Sentences:

1. Once something happened.

2. What happened was that his back happened to be half turned.

3. His back was half turned toward the door.

4. During this time he heard a noise there.

5. Upon hearing the noise, he wheeled.

6. Also upon hearing the noise, he sprang up.

7. While wheeling and springing up, he was doing something else.

8. He was uttering a cry.

9. The cry was loud.

---

1. Model: Silently, desperately, he fought with all his weapons.

Katherine Anne Porter, Ship of Fools

2. Model: Because of the rain, the windows were shut tight, and the air was getting muggy.

Robert R. McCammon, Boy's Life

3. Model: Ahead, Grant saw an island, rugged and craggy, rising sharply from the ocean.

Michael Crichton, Jurassic Park

4. Model: The fixer got up on his raw hands and bleeding knees and went on, blindly crawling across the yard.

Bernard Malamud, The Fixer

5. Model: Finally, she closed the miniblinds, got up from the chair, and went downstairs to make herself a western omelet.

Terry McMillan, Waiting to Exhale

Practice 2

The model sentences in this practice are longer. Take each long model sentence and express the content in shorter sentences.

Example

Model: He backed Jack up against the ropes, measured him and then hooked the left very light to the side of Jack's head and socked the right into the body as hard as he could sock, just as low as he could get it.

Ernest Hemingway, "Fifty Grand"

Shorter Sentences:

1. He backed Jack up.

2. He backed him up against the ropes.

3. He then did several more things.

4. He measured Jack.

5. Then he hooked the left.

6. The hooking was very light.

7. The hooking was to the side of the head.

8. The head was Jack's.

9. Next he socked the right.

10. He socked it into the body of Jack.

11. The socking was hard.

12. It was as hard as he could sock.

13. The socking was also low.

14. It was just as low as he could get it.

---

1. Model: On the table, covered with oilcloth figured with clusters of blue grapes, a place was set, and he smelled hot coffee-cake of some kind.

   Willa Cather, "Neighbor Rosicky"

2. Model: Every old woman was a doctor, and gathered her own medicines in the woods, and knew how to compound doses that would stir the vitals of a cast-iron dog.

   Mark Twain, Mark Twain's Autobiography

3. Model: She cleared away the smoking things, then drew back the cotton bedspread from the bed she had been sitting on, took off her slippers, and got into bed.

   J. D. Salinger, Franny and Zooey

4. Model: The driver of the car stopped it, slamming it to a skidding halt on the greasy pavement without warning, actually flinging the two passengers forward until they caught themselves with their braced hands against the dash.

   William Faulkner, "Delta Autumn"

5. Model: The first wave carried with it men accustomed to spaces and coldness and being alone, the coyote and cattlemen, with no fat on them, with faces the years had worn the flesh off, with eyes like nailheads, and hands like the material of old gloves, ready to touch anything.

   Ray Bradbury, The Martian Chronicles

Practice 3

Without looking back at the model sentences in Practices 1 and 2, use your lists of short sentences from those practices to combine back into single sentences. Finally, compare your single sentences with the original model sentences in Practices 1 and 2.

Activity 22

Combining Then Imitating

Practice 1

Combine the pairs of sentences into just one sentence by making the underlined portion part of the first sentence. Decide where the part fits most smoothly into the first sentence. Add commas to punctuate the part you insert into the first sentence.

Next, write an imitation of the sentence you produce, using your own content but the structure of that sentence.

Example

Pair: Mrs. Harding disciplined us for handing in messy notebooks. She was <u>our fifth-grade teacher</u>.

Combined: Mrs. Harding, <u>our fifth-grade teacher</u>, disciplined us for handing in messy notebooks.

Joyce Carol Oates, Haunted

Imitation: Jack Kempner, their soccer coach, congratulated the team for winning their toughest game.

Adding Words:

1. They burst out of the clouds into a shaft of light. All of this happened <u>abruptly</u>.

   Madeleine L'Engle, A Wrinkle in Time

2. She was in the doorway. She was <u>excited and afraid</u>.

   John Christopher, The Guardians

3. Thomas ate two portions of meat, nothing else. He was <u>hungry</u>.

   Hal Borland, When the Legends Die

4. He began to angle toward the valley. He did this <u>warily, slowly</u>.

   Alexander Key, The Forgotten Door

5. He was a mean-looking man. He was <u>red in the face and bearded</u>.

          Mildred D. Taylor, Roll of Thunder, Hear My Cry

Adding Phrases:

6. He lowered his eyes. He did this <u>to hide the tears</u>.

          Bill and Vera Cleaver, Where the Lilies Bloom

7. He ate slowly. As he ate, he was <u>hoping that in days to come he'd be able to remember how good each mouthful had been</u>.

          Irene Hunt, Across Five Aprils

8. The birds migrated early from the Great Marsh. The migration was <u>in the spring of 1940</u>.

          Paul Gallico, The Snow Goose

9. He then buried his face in his hands and cried. He was <u>totally dismayed by what had happened</u>.

          Mildred D. Taylor, Roll of Thunder, Hear My Cry

10. The meat hung in the smoke-house. It was <u>dry-cured for the feeding of the dogs</u>.

          Marjorie Kinnan Rawlings, The Yearling

Adding Clauses:

11. Gwydion caught sight of them instantly. He was someone <u>whose eyes were everywhere at once</u>.

          Lloyd Alexander, The Book of Three

12. She rose from the table. The table was <u>where she was sitting</u>.

          Cormac McCarthy, All the Pretty Horses

13. By afternoon, Perrault returned with three more dogs. He was the one <u>who was in a hurry to be on the trail to Dawson</u>.

          Jack London, The Call of the Wild

14. They believed him. This happened <u>when Fiver said the iron tree was harmless</u>.

          Richard Adams, Watership Down

15. He looked like the total all-American kid. This impression occurred <u>as he pedaled his twenty-six-inch Schwinn with the apehanger handlebars up the residential suburban street</u>.

Stephen King, "Apt Pupil" from Different Seasons

Practice 2

Combine the sets of sentences into one sentence by making the underlined portions parts of the first sentence. Decide where the parts fit most smoothly into the first sentence. Add commas to punctuate the sentence parts you insert.

Next, write an imitation of the sentence you produce, using your own content but the structure of that sentence.

Example

Set: The Horned King rode to the wicker baskets and thrust the fire into them. He did this <u>before Gwydion could speak again</u>. The Horned King was <u>bearing a torch</u>.

Combined: Before Gwydion could speak again, the Horned King, bearing a torch, rode to the wicker baskets and thrust the fire into them.

Lloyd Alexander, The Book of Three

Imitation: As the hitter darted toward first base, the pitcher, aiming with precision, threw the ball to the first base player and got the ball into the sweet spot.

---

1. Aunt Dorothy was waiting at the front door with her own small daughter. Aunt Dorothy was <u>tall and bony</u>. Her daughter was <u>Diane</u>.

Robert Lipsyte, The Contender

2. There was a huge moulting stuffed moose head. It was <u>in the dining hall</u>. It was <u>over the stone fireplace that was never used</u>. The moose head was something <u>which looked somehow carnivorous</u>.

Margaret Atwood, Wilderness Tips

3. Craig sat and waited for his father to tell him what he should do next. Craig was <u>calm now, at peace</u>. He sat and waited <u>just as he had done so many times as a child</u>.

   Stephen King, "The Langoliers"

4. Perhaps an elderly gentleman lived there. He lived there <u>alone</u>. He was <u>someone who had known her grandfather</u>. He was <u>someone who had visited the Parrs in Cummington</u>.

   Joyce Carol Oates, "The Doll" from Haunted

5. The lawyer lay on an old Army cot. The cot was <u>in the closed anteroom</u>. It was one <u>he kept there for naps</u>. There was <u>a newspaper folded over his face as though he were a corpse being protected from flies</u>.

   Frank Bonham, Chief

Activity 23

Combining Effectively

Practice 1

Each pair lists sentences resulting from several sentences combined into one. Choose the more effective sentence in each pair and explain why it's more effective. The more effective sentence is the original sentence by the professional writer.

Example

a. The carpenter wanted to talk about building a platform to raise the bed with the writer, so he, who had been a soldier in the Civil War, came into the writer's room and sat down.

b. The carpenter, who had been a soldier in the Civil War, came into the writer's room and sat down to talk about building a platform to raise the bed.

More Effective Version: *b*

Reasons: The first version wastes words, and is confusing because it sounds as if the writer would be in the bed while the carpenter was building the platform. The second sentence, from *Winesburg, Ohio* by Sherwood Anderson, avoids these problems.

1a. The boy watched, his eyes bulging in the dark.

b. While his eyes were bulging in the dark, the boy watched.

2a. One of the dogs had disappeared, which was the best one.

b. One of the dogs, the best one, had disappeared.

3a. The country house, on this particular wintry afternoon, was most enjoyable.

b. Most enjoyable was, on this particular afternoon in winter, the house in the country.

4a. Its attacker was bitten by the dying animal on the neck only after the dying animal had snarled, lifted its head, and twisted.

  b. The dying animal snarled, and suddenly lifted its head and twisted, sinking its teeth into the neck of its attacker.

5a. Men slept in bunks or hammocks so tightly squeezed together that the reclining bodies looked like slabs of meat packed for the market wagons.

  b. They looked like slabs of meat that were being packed for the wagons going to the market, these men who slept in bunks or hammocks and were so tightly squeezed together.

Practice 2

Combine each list of sentences twice to produce two different sentences. Tell which sentence is more effective and why.

1a. He moves nervously.

  b. He moves fast.

  c. His movement, however, has a restraint.

  d. The restraint suggests that he is a cautious man.

  e. The restraint suggests that he is a thoughtful man.
           Based on a sentence by John Hersey, Hiroshima

2a. The girls stood aside.

  b. The very small children rolled in the dust.

  c. Some children clung to the hands of their older brothers or sisters.

  d. The girls were doing two things.

  e. They looked over their shoulders at the boys.

  f. They talked among themselves.
          Based on a sentence by Shirley Jackson, "The Lottery"

3a. The cake was shaped in a frying pan.

b. He took flour.

c. He took oil.

d. He shaped them into a cake.

e. The stove functioned on gas.

f. The gas was bottled.

g. He lighted the stove.

h. The stove was little.

> *Based on a sentence by Albert Camus, "The Guest,"*
> *from* Exile and the Kingdom

4a. He set the cake on the windowsill.

b. The purpose was to cool it.

c. He did this after the cake was done.

d. He heated some milk.

e. The milk was condensed.

f. The milk was diluted with water.

g. He beat up the eggs.

h. The eggs were beaten into an omelette.

> *Based on a sentence by Albert Camus, "The Guest,"*
> *from* Exile and the Kingdom

5a. One of the travelers napped upon his cane.

b. The napping was done fitfully.

c. The traveler was the fifth traveler.

d. He sat across the aisle.

e. He sat next to the middle door there.

f. He was a gentleman.

g. He was old.

h. He was withered.

> *Based on a sentence by Henry Sydnor Harrison, "Miss Hinch"*

Practice 3

Write five short sentences that begin with the same subject. Combine the sentences in two different ways that are effective.

Example

Subject: recorded sound

Five Sentences with Same Subject:

1. Recorded sound was once primitive compared to today's quality.

2. Recorded sound began as monaural sound.

3. Recorded sound added the illusion of a third dimension through two-track stereo.

4. Recorded sound is now possible in four channels, called quadraphonic sound.

5. Recorded sound today almost duplicates the sound of a live performance.

Sample Effective Combinations:

a. Once primitive compared to today's quality, recorded sound, which began as monaural, added the illusion of a third dimension through stereo, and more recently became available in four channels, called quadraphonic, that almost duplicates the sound of a live performance.

b. Although today almost duplicating the sound of a live performance through quadraphonic recording, recorded sound was once primitive compared to today's quality, monaural sound, which then evolved into stereo, an illusion of a third dimension.

Activity 24

Combining Economically

Practice 1

Combine each list into just one sentence. The number of words in the professional writer's original sentence is indicated. Don't worry about using that exact number, but try not to exceed it by much.

1a. Now the sky was without a cloud.

  b. It was pale blue.

  c. It was delicate.

  d. It was luminous.

  e. It was scintillating with morning.

Word Count: fourteen

Frank Norris, The Octopus

2a. He distributed handbills for merchants.

  b. He did this, and the following activities, from ages ten to fifteen.

  c. He held horses.

  d. He ran confidential errands.

Word Count: fifteen

Thornton Wilder, The Bridge of San Luis Rey

3a. Nick looked down into the water.

  b. The water was clear.

  c. The water was brown.

  d. The brown color came from the pebbly bottom.

  e. As Nick looked down he watched the trout.

  f. The trout were keeping themselves steady in the current.

g. They kept themselves steady with their fins.

h. Their fins were wavering.

Word Count: twenty-five

Ernest Hemingway, "Big Two-Hearted River"

4a. On one side was a tiny meadow.

b. The meadow began at the very lip of the pool.

c. The meadow had a surface of green.

d. The surface was cool.

e. The surface was resilient.

f. The surface extended.

g. The surface extended to the base.

h. The base was of the browning wall.

Word Count: thirty

Jack London, "All Gold Canyon"

5a. He turned on the TV.

b. He found a game on the TV.

c. The game was a Cincinnati-Boston exhibition baseball game.

d. The game was wending its slow way.

e. The slow way was into the eighth inning.

f. He lay down on the sofa.

g. He did this to watch the game.

h. And then he almost immediately dozed off.

Word Count: thirty-three

Stephen King, "The Library Policemen"

Practice 2

Imitate the sentences you produced in Practice 1, using your own content but the structures of those sentences.

Example

Sentences to Be Combined

1. One day when I went out to my woodpile, something happened.

2. What happened was that I observed two ants.

3. They were both large.

4. One was red.

5. The other was the much larger of the two ants.

6. This larger one was nearly half an inch long.

7. This larger one was black.

8. The two ants were fiercely contending with one another.

Sample Combination

One day when I went out to my woodpile, I observed two large ants, the one red, the other much larger, fiercely contending with one another.

Henry David Thoreau, Walden

Imitation: The time when our team went to Florida, we travelled all over the state, our schedule hectic, our itinerary full, competing with teams from all over the country.

Activity 25

Combining Sentences in Paragraphs

Practice 1

Each list of sentences can be combined to make one sentence of a paragraph. Combine each list into one sentence. The number of words in the professional writer's original sentences are indicated. Don't worry about using that exact number, but try not to exceed it by much.

When you finish, compare your sentences to the sentences by the professional writers in the References section. If your sentences aren't as good, learn why. If yours are as good or better, congratulations! You're writing like a pro.

Description of a Snail Shell adapted from Anne Morrow Lindbergh, *Gift from the Sea*

1a. This is a snail shell.

  b. It is round.

  c. It is full.

  d. It is glossy.

  e. The gloss is like a horse chestnut.

Word Count: thirteen (short sentence)

2a. The shell is comfortable.

  b. The shell is compact.

  c. It sits curled up.

  d. It sits in the hollow of my hand.

  e. It sits curled up like a cat.

Word Count: sixteen (medium sentence)

3a. It is milky.

  b. It is opaque.

  c. It has a pinkish bloom.

d. The bloom is like the sky on an evening.

e. The evening is in summer.

f. The evening sky is ripening.

g. The ripening is to rain.

Word Count: eighteen (medium sentence)

4a. A spiral is pencilled on its face.

b. The face is smooth.

c. The face is symmetrical.

d. The spiral is pencilled with precision.

e. The spiral winds inward to the center.

f. The center is a pinpoint.

g. The pinpoint is of the center of the shell.

h. The center is the core.

i. The core is tiny.

j. The core is of the apex.

k. The core is the pupil of the eye.

Word Count: thirty-two (long sentence)

5a. It stares at me.

b. It is this mysterious eye.

c. I stare back.

Word Count: eleven (short sentence)

Narration of a Bullfight adapted from Ernest Hemingway, "The Undefeated"

1a. Manuel waved his hand.

b. Manuel was leaning against the barrera.

c. Manuel was watching the bull.

    d. And the gypsy ran out.

    e. The gypsy was trailing his cape.

Word Count: nineteen (medium sentence)

2a. The bull pivoted and charged the cape.

    b. The bull was in full gallop.

    c. The bull's head was down.

    d. The bull's tail was rising.

Word Count: sixteen (medium sentence)

3a. The gypsy moved.

    b. The movement was in a zigzag.

    c. And as he passed, the bull caught sight of him.

    d. The bull abandoned the cape.

    e. The reason for the abandonment was to charge the man.

Word Count: twenty-four (medium sentence)

4a. The gypsy sprinted and vaulted the red fence.

    b. The red fence was of the barrera.

    c. As the gypsy sprinted and vaulted, the bull struck something.

    d. The bull struck the red fence of the barrera.

    e. The bull struck it with his horns.

Word Count: nineteen (medium sentence)

5a. He tossed into it with his horns.

    b. He tossed into it twice.

    c. He was banging into the wood.

    d. He was banging blindly.

Word Count: twelve (short sentence)

Practice 2

Each list of sentences can be combined to make the sentences of a paragraph. Unlike the last practice in which sentence breaks were indicated, this time you must decide where the sentences break. The number of words in the professional writer's original paragraphs are indicated. Don't worry about using that exact number, but try not to exceed it by much.

When you finish each paragraph, compare your paragraphs to the paragraphs by the professional writers in the References section.

Description of a Victorian House adapted from Ray Bradbury, *The Martian Chronicles* (Length of Paragraph: WORDS: 92, SENTENCES: 4)

1. An iron deer stood.

2. It stood outside.

3. It stood upon this lawn.

4. A Victorian house stood further up on the green.

5. The house was tall.

6. The house was brown.

7. The house was quiet in the sunlight.

8. The house was all covered with scrolls and rococo.

9. The house's windows were made of blue colored glass.

10. The house's windows were made of pink colored glass.

11. The house's windows were made of yellow colored glass.

12. The house's windows were made of green colored glass.

13. Two things were upon the porch.

14. One was geraniums.

15. The geraniums were hairy.

16. The other was a swing.

17. The swing was old.

18. The swing was hooked into the porch ceiling.

19. The swing now swung back and forth, back and forth.

20. The swinging occurred in a little breeze.

21. A cupola was at the summit of the house.

22. The cupola had diamond leaded-glass windows.

23. The cupola had a dunce-cap roof!

Narration of a Hunting Accident adapted from Saki, "The Interlopers" (Length of Paragraph: WORDS: 160, SENTENCES: 5)

1. Ulrich von Gradwitz found himself stretched on the ground.

2. One arm was beneath him.

3. It was numb.

4. The other was held almost as helplessly.

5. This arm was held in a tight tangle of forked branches.

6. Both legs were pinned beneath the fallen mass.

7. His heavy shooting boots had saved his feet.

8. The boots had saved the feet from being crushed to pieces.

9. His fractures were not as serious as they might have been.

10. It was evident, however, that he could not move.

11. He could not move from his present position.

12. He could not move from there till someone came to release him.

13. The descending twigs had slashed the skin.

14. The skin was of his face.

15. He had to wink away some drops of blood from his eyelids.

16. He had to do this before he could take in a general view.

17. The general view was of the disaster.

18. Someone lay at his side.

19. The someone was so near.

20. Under normal circumstances he could almost have touched him.

21. Georg Znaeym was that someone.

22. Georg was alive.

23. Georg was struggling.

24. Georg was obviously, however, as helplessly pinioned down as himself.

25. All round them lay wreckage.

26. The wreckage was thick-strewn.

27. The wreckage was of splintered branches.

28. The wreckage was of broken twigs.

*A*ctivity 26

Combining to Revise

Practice 1

Revise each paragraph by combining sentences. The result will be fewer words and fewer sentences but increased sentence variety and maturity.

Narration of a Snowy School Day

(1) The weather report the night before mentioned the possibility of four to six inches of snow. (2) The snow was supposed to start either during the night or early the next morning. (3) I fell asleep and hoped that school would be cancelled. (4) School was usually cancelled when it snowed that much. (5) I awoke the next morning. (6) The sky was very cloudy, but there was no snow, not even a flake. (7) Reluctantly I got dressed. (8) I then ate breakfast. (9) I got in my car and drove toward school. (10) Just before I got there, the snow started. (11) When I entered school, everyone was talking about whether we would be let out of school because of the snow. (12) Nobody was very enthused about being in school that morning. (13) The students weren't. (14) The teachers weren't either. (15) The principal was standing in the cafeteria looking out the window. (16) He wasn't either. (17) The snow continued coming down heavily for about two more hours. (18) Finally, during social studies class, the principal came on the intercom. (19) He announced that school would close early because of the snow. (20) We were dismissed about twenty minutes later.

Description of a Driver's Test

(1) I was very nervous before my driving test. (2) I had a hard time sleeping the night before. (3) I kept going over the answers to the questions in the little driver's manual they had given me to study from. (4) I was still nervous in the test room at the Department of Motor Vehicles. (5) There were about twenty others there to take their tests. (6) Most were young, about my age. (7) There was one man who looked almost sixty. (8) He had on glasses that were the thickest I had ever

seen. (9) When he spoke to ask one of the clerks where the rest room was, I noticed his foreign accent. (10) He probably knew how to drive. (11) He probably had learned in his native country. (12) He had to take the test here though to get a license in our country. (13) A middle-age woman, who was well dressed, sat two desks down from me. (14) She added to my nervousness. (15) She was talking to a girl next to her. (16) She told the girl that this part of the examination was easy. (17) She meant the written test part, not the driving part. (18) She told the girl that she had taken the drivers' examination four times. (19) Each time she had passed the written part, but not the driving part. (20) She had never passed the driving part. (21) Once she had an accident. (22) She backed into the parked car owned by the commissioner of motor vehicles. (23) Another time she jumped a curb. (24) Another time she took too long to parallel park. (25) And another time she got so tense that she started crying and could not continue.

Practice 2

Select two paragraphs from your own writing to revise by combining sentences. Aim for fewer words and sentences but increased sentence maturity and variety.

Sentence combining is an easy, effective revision strategy you can use with almost everything you write to improve your writing.

4

Sentence Expanding

Sentence expanding changes sentences into sentences like those of professional writers. In these sentence expanding practices, you are given a part of a sentence by a professional writer, and then you add your own sentence parts (expansions) to that sentence. You become a partner with a professional writer, working together to compose sentences.

All of the sentences you will expand are based on sentences written by professional writers. In expanding sentences, pay attention to how these writers composed their sentences. Apply what you learn to your own sentences.

Activity 27

Expanding with Words

Practice 1

One way to expand sentences is to add either single words or a series of two or more similar words. Model sentences 1–5 contain examples of single words (underlined); 6–10 contain examples of series. Study the model sentences and then write an imitation of each, using your own content but the structure of the model.

Example

Model (Single Word): <u>Ahead</u>, Taran heard a thrashing among the leaves.

Lloyd Alexander, The Book of Three

Imitation: <u>Quickly</u>, Bob got some bait for the hook.

Model (Series of Words): I gazed at the pond, <u>gray</u> and <u>calm</u>, until she was ready to go on.

Mildred D. Taylor, Roll of Thunder, Hear My Cry

Imitation: Delvon played with the puppy, <u>frisky</u> and <u>yappy</u>, when he was looking for something to do.

---

1. <u>Outside</u>, he murmured to himself.

   William H. Armstrong, Sounder

2. I jumped to my feet, <u>thunderstruck</u>.

   Antoine de Saint-Exupéry, The Little Prince

3. <u>Alone</u>, Tom looked around the room and knew he was a stranger.

   Hal Borland, When the Legends Die

4. Gwydion sat upright, <u>tense</u> as a bowstring.

   Lloyd Alexander, The Book of Three

5. Always <u>neat</u>, six-year-old Little Man never allowed dirt or tears or stains to mar anything he owned.

Mildred D. Taylor, Roll of Thunder, Hear My Cry

6. Someone was humming under her breath, <u>high</u> and <u>sweet</u>.

Ray Bradbury, The Martian Chronicles

7. <u>Quickly</u> and <u>noisily</u>, Gerard came in.

Elizabeth Bowen, "Foothold"

8. She was in the doorway, <u>excited</u> and <u>afraid</u>.

John Christopher, The Guardians

9. Spitz, <u>cold</u> and <u>calculating</u>, even in his supreme moods, left the pack and cut across a narrow neck of land where the creek made a long bend around.

Jack London, The Call of the Wild

10. In the utter silence of that night some outside sound woke me and I got up and looked out across the frozen glitter and saw a gray fox sitting on our fence, <u>wild</u>, <u>tattered</u>, and <u>hungry-looking</u>.

Bill and Vera Cleaver, Where the Lilies Bloom

Practice 2

Expand the following sentences by adding a single word, or a series of similar words, at the slash mark (/). Also, to familiarize yourself with how professionals write, copy the sentences.

1. The man was about fifty, /.

Frank Bonham, Chief

2. /, the gust of wind threw sand against the side of the car.

Stephen King, Desperation

3. Templeton, /, heard the commotion and awoke.

E. B. White, Charlotte's Web

4. Bea is a fine-looking woman, /, with rich brown skin and thick black hair.

Eugenia Collier, "Sweet Potato Pie"

5. We all remembered someone, and I remembered my father, /.

   Scott O'Dell, Island of the Blue Dolphins

6. Laughter, / , filled the room.

   Rosa Guy, The Friends

7. / , he wandered about the many tents, only to find that one place was as cold as another.

   Jack London, The Call of the Wild

8. / , they drove through the darkness, and though the rain stopped, the wind rushed by and whistled and made strange sounds.

   Frances Hodgson Burnett, The Secret Garden

9. Hattie sat down at her old Spanish table, watching them in the cloudy warmth of the day, clasping her hands, / .

   Saul Bellow, "Leaving the Yellow House"

10. Beyond Romey's slight figure I saw this tree, / , its branches all streamed back in one direction from the winds that had battered it year after year.

    Bill and Vera Cleaver, Where the Lilies Bloom

Activity 28

Expanding with Phrases (Part One)

Practice 1

A second way to expand sentences is to add phrases. A phrase is a sentence part made up of more than one word. The model sentences contain examples of different kinds of phrases: *appositive*, *absolute*, and *infinitive*. Some sentences contain single phrases, and others contain a series of two or more of the same kind of phrase. Study the model sentences, especially the different kinds of phrases underlined. Then write an imitation of each, using your own content but the structure of the model.

Example

Model (Single Phrase): He signaled to Jake, <u>the middle brother</u>, to take over the cash register.

Robert Lipsyte, The Contender

Imitation: The principal called to Jimmy, <u>the class president</u>, to run the meeting.

Model (Series of Similar Phrases): After a minute, two of the creatures, <u>a doe</u> and <u>her fawn</u>, moved hesitantly down the slope and stood looking at him curiously.

Alexander Key, The Forgotten Door

Imitation: During the movie, two people, <u>a father</u> and <u>his little boy</u>, applauded wildly for the hero and started cheering at the end.

Appositive Phrases

Appositive phrases are sentence parts that identify persons, places, or things. They usually begin with *a*, *an*, or *the*. They answer these questions: Who is this person? What is this place? What is this thing?

1. Tomorrow is Wednesday, <u>a working day</u>. (single appositive phrase)

   Robert Lipsyte, The Contender

2. The face of Liliana Methol, <u>the fifth woman in the plane</u>, was badly bruised and covered with blood. (single appositive phrase)

   Piers Paul Read, Alive

3. There was something similar about them in that moment, <u>the same oval face</u>, <u>the same round brown eyes</u>, <u>the same brown hair hanging over the forehead</u>, <u>the same freckles on the nose</u>. (series of appositive phrases)

   Betsy Byars, The Summer of the Swans

Absolute Phrases

Absolute phrases are sentence parts that would be complete sentences if you added *was* or *were* within the absolute phrase. Most absolute phrases begin with *my, his, her, its, our,* or *their.*

4. <u>His fingers</u> [were] <u>smarting</u>, the shamefaced Taran hurried from the cottage and found Coll near the vegetable garden. (single absolute phrase)

   Lloyd Alexander, The Book of Three

5. Big, rough teen-agers jostled through the crowd, <u>their sleeves</u> [were] <u>rolled high enough to show off blue and red tattoos</u>. (single absolute phrase)

   Robert Lipsyte, The Contender

6. He waited, <u>his eyes</u> [were] <u>open</u>, <u>his senses</u> [were] <u>alert</u>. (series of absolute phrases)

   Hal Borland, When the Legends Die

7. I found Aunt Loma sitting at the kitchen table, <u>her long curly red hair</u> [was] <u>still loose and tousled</u>, <u>her dirty breakfast dishes</u> [were] <u>pushed back to clear a space</u>. (series of absolute phrases)

   Olive Ann Burns, Cold Sassy Tree

Infinitive Phrases

Infinitive phrases are sentence parts that always begin with *to* followed by a verb: for example, *to sing, to read, to linger, to laugh, to sigh, to study*, etc.

8. <u>To hide the tears</u>, he lowered his eyes. (single infinitive phrase)
   Bill and Vera Cleaver, Where the Lilies Bloom

9. She thought of only one thing, <u>to keep him from leaving the box</u>. (single infinitive phrase)
   Gaston Leroux, The Phantom of the Opera

10. <u>To rest, to eat Meo's beans and chili, to wait for spring and a new season</u>, they went home. (series of infinitive phrases)
    Hal Borland, When the Legends Die

Practice 2

Expand the following sentences by adding a single phrase, or a series of phrases, at the slash mark (/). Use the type of phrase in parentheses. Then check the References section to see the original phrases. Also, to familiarize yourself with how professionals write, copy the sentences.

1. / , he took little interest in troublesome things, preferring to remain on good terms with everyone. (appositive phrase)
   Mildred D. Taylor, Roll of Thunder, Hear My Cry

2. I looked out across the ravaged fields and saw Romey, / , moving around in Roy Luther's garden. (appositive phrase)
   Bill and Vera Cleaver, Where the Lilies Bloom

3. The real estate agent, / , soon joined them. (appositive phrase)
   Willa Cather, "The Sculptor's Funeral"

4. There they were in the schoolroom again, / and / and /. (series of appositive phrases)
   Meindert DeJong, The Wheel on the School

5. I could see Lestat feeling along the brick walls, / . (absolute phrase)

Anne Rice, Interview with the Vampire

6. On impulse, he went in, bought a bag of gumdrops, and went on up the street, / . (absolute phrase)

Hal Borland, When the Legends Die

7. Slowly, / and / , he lifted the truck in one fluid, powerful motion until the front was several inches off the ground and slowly walked it to the left of the road, where he set it down as gently as a sleeping child. (series of absolute phrases)

Mildred D. Taylor, Roll of Thunder, Hear My Cry

8. / , he lowered his head, resting it against the wall and reached up with his hands, feeling all over the stone above him. (infinitive phrase)

Robb White, Deathwatch

9. Slowly, I crawled on, stopping to listen, / , / . (series of infinitive phrases)

Scott O'Dell, Island of the Blue Dolphins

10. He knew the bears would soon be leaving their winter dens, / , / , / , and / . (series of infinitive phrases)

Hal Borland, When the Legends Die

Activity 29

Expanding with Phrases (Part Two)

Practice 1

Here are three more phrases you can use to expand sentences: *prepositional*, *participial*, and *past participial*. Some sentences contain single phrases; others contain a series of two or more of the same kind of phrase. Study the model sentences, especially the different kinds of phrases underlined. Then write an imitation of each, using your own content but the structure of the model.

Prepositional Phrases
Prepositional phrases are sentence parts that begin with words like *in*, *near*, *on*, *after*, *before*, *by*, *of*, *during*, *with*, and *for*. Some prepositional phrases tell where things happen: in the barn, by the school. Some tell when: after the dance, before the game, during the morning. Others tell what kind of person: the man in the dirty Levis, the woman with a red dress. Some tell what kind of place: store in the new mall, road near the covered bridge. Others tell what kind of thing: season of the year, game for little kids.

1. After breakfast, Billy got out his best knife, the one with a needle point. (two prepositional phrases)
   John Steinbeck, The Red Pony

2. By the end of the first round, his face felt as if it had been stung by a hundred bees. (three prepositional phrases)
   Robert Lipsyte, The Contender

3. Over the river and through the woods, to Grandmother's house we go. (three prepositional phrases)
   Anonymous

Participial Phrases
Participial phrases are sentence parts that always begin with an *ing* word. They describe people, places, or things mentioned in the sentence they appear in.

4. It went slowly down the road, <u>taking its time</u>. (single participial phrase)
   Brian W. Aldiss, "Who Can Replace a Man?"

5. <u>Taking the stairs two at a time</u>, he didn't even notice me following behind. (single participial phrase)
   Olive Anne Burns, Cold Sassy Tree

6. I spent the entire day in a sulk, <u>staring out the window, waiting for the rain to stop</u>. (series of participial phrases)
   Rosa Guy, The Friends

Past Participial Phrases

Past participial phrases are sentence parts that usually begin with words that end in *ed* or *en. Covering* is a present participle; *covered* is a past participle. *Forgiving* is a present participle; *forgiven* is past. Like present participial phrases, they describe people, places, or things mentioned in the sentence they appear in.

7. <u>Pursued by killer whales</u>, the bass had tried to escape by swimming toward shore. (single past participial phrase)
   Joseph Krumgold, Onion John

8. The exercise got the blood pumping through his brain, <u>numbed by the hours of lost sleep</u>. (single past participial phrase)
   Frank Bonham, Chief

9. Taran, <u>hunched against a tree root</u>, was pulling his cloak closer around his shoulders. (single past participial phrase)
   Lloyd Alexander, The Book of Three

10. Their heads were covered with wigs of European hair, <u>curled in the latest fashion</u>, and <u>adorned with ropes of pearls, rubies, and diamonds</u>. (series of past participial phrases)
    Margaret Landon, Anna and the King of Siam

Practice 2

Expand the following sentences by adding a single phrase, or a series of phrases, at the slash mark (/). Use the type of phrase in parentheses. Then check the References section to see the original phrases. Also, to familiarize yourself with how professionals write, copy the sentences.

1. / , a woman sang. (prepositional phrase)
   Ray Bradbury, The Martian Chronicles

2. / , warriors on high stilts beat upraised swords against their shields. (prepositional phrase)
   Lloyd Alexander, The Book of Three

3. / , / , / , the boy followed the dog, whose anxious pace slowed from age as they went. (series of prepositional phrases)
   William Armstrong, Sounder

4. Mary asked no more questions but waited in the darkness of her corner, / . (participial phrase)
   Frances Hodgson Burnett, The Secret Garden

5. A large woman, / , got out and waddled over to them. (participial phrase)
   Alexander Key, The Forgotten Door

6. Ima Dean, with a huge bag of yellow and red wrapped candies, was sitting on the floor, / , / . (series of participial phrases)
   Bill and Vera Cleaver, Where the Lilies Bloom

7. They were standing there in front of the locked door in the nearly empty plane, / , when the man in the red shirt and the man in the crew-necked jersey arrived, / . (two participial phrases in different places)
   Stephen King, The Langoliers

8. He walked on, / . (past participial phrase)
   Robert Lipsyte, The Contender

9. / , he held his temples desperately with both hands and was wretchedly sick. (past participial phrase)
   Bill and Vera Cleaver, Where the Lilies Bloom

10. He was a broad, bandy-legged little man with a walrus mustache, with square hands, / and / . (series of past participial phrases)
    John Steinbeck, The Red Pony

Activity 30

Expanding with Clauses (Part One)

Practice 1

Another way to expand sentences is to add clauses. A clause is a sentence part made up of several words including a subject and verb.

The model sentences below contain examples of adjective clauses. Study the model sentences and then write an imitation of each, using your own content but the structure of the model.

Adjective Clauses

Adjective clauses are sentence parts that often begin with *who* or *which*. Adjective clauses give more information about a noun to the left of the clause.

Example

Model (adjective clause): My hands were wrapped in an old towel, <u>which I also used to wipe the sweat from my face</u>.

Richard E. Kim, Lost Names

Imitation: The wall was covered with a climbing vine, <u>which the owners planted long ago to conceal cracks in the bricks</u>.

---

1. He put the big bloody heart, <u>which was still beating</u>, into her hands.

   Willard Price, The Killer Shark

2. The taxi driver, <u>who had not yet been paid</u>, carefully placed Miss Hearne in the back seat of his car and started the engine.

   Brian Moore, The Lonely Passion of Judith Hearne

3. Lily was still wearing her wedding sandals, <u>which had begun to blister her</u>.

   Joan Aiken, "Searching for Summer"

4. He reached the fruit and dropped it to the third boy, <u>who stood below holding out his coat as a blanket</u>.

    Christy Brown, My Left Foot

5. The women, <u>who were never asked to do more than stay at home, cook food, and make clothing</u>, now must take the place of the men and face the dangers, <u>which abound beyond the village</u>. (two adjective clauses)

    Scott O'Dell, Island of the Blue Dolphins

Practice 2

Expand the sentences by adding an adjective clause at the slash mark (/). Also, to familiarize yourself with how professionals write, copy the sentences.

1. Red, /, was the one who died penniless.

    Hal Borland, When the Legends Die

2. They had planned to spend the first night at Bardstown, /.

    Peter Taylor, "Reservations: A Love Story"

3. She also had to watch our three chickens, / .

    Laurence Yep, Dragonwings

4. Boysie, / , heard the door shut and came to the living room.

    Betsy Byars, The Summer of the Swans

5. Ramo was standing on one foot and then the other, watching the ship coming, / .

    Scott O'Dell, Island of the Blue Dolphins

Activity 31

Expanding with Clauses (Part Two)

Practice 1

The model sentences below contain examples of adverb clauses. Study the model sentences and then write an imitation of each, using your own content but the structure of the model.

Adverb Clauses

Adverb clauses are sentence parts that usually begin with *when*, *as*, *since*, *before*, or *after*. Adverb clauses tell when something mentioned in the sentence happened.

Example

Model (adverb clause): <u>When the general had gone</u>, Rainsford took up his flight again.

Richard Connell, "The Most Dangerous Game"

Imitation: <u>When the newspaper had landed</u>, the dog retrieved it obediently.

---

1. <u>When he reached the dining room</u>, he sat down at a table near a window.

   Willa Cather, "Paul's Case"

2. Benny caught the boy by the shoulder <u>before he could run to the bear</u>, which was bawling and snapping at the chain.

   Hal Borland, When the Legends Die

3. The gwythaints, which at a distance had seemed no more than dry leaves in the wind, grew larger and larger, <u>as they plunged toward horse and riders</u>.

   Lloyd Alexander, The Book of Three

4. Every morning, <u>after Jody had curried and brushed the pony</u>, he let down the barrier of the stall, and the pony

thrust past him and raced down the barn and into the corral.

John Steinbeck, The Red Pony

5. Shrinking is always more painful than growing, <u>since for a moment all your bones jam together like a crowd on market day</u>, but the pain was over quickly enough <u>as I became the size of a cat</u>. (two adverb clauses)

Laurence Yep, Dragon of the Lost Sea

Practice 2

Expand the following sentences by adding an adverb clause at the slash mark (/). Also, to familiarize yourself with how professionals write, copy the sentences.

1. We passed two children, sobbing and moaning / .

Peter Abrahams, Tell Freedom

2. / , I set the cream puffs on the coffee table and stood back looking at them.

Rosa Guy, Edith Jackson

3. In the winter, / , I hate the mountains.

Bill and Vera Cleaver, Where the Lilies Bloom

4. Dicey was up and dressed, washed and fed, and out the door, with the day's work outlined in her head, / .

Cynthia Voigt, Seventeen Against the Dealer

5. / , / , the boy or the father took a hammer with a homemade handle, went to the flat rock, and cracked as many walnuts as could be kerneled in a night. (series of adverb clauses)

William H. Armstrong, Sounder

*A*ctivity 32

Reviewing Expansions in Sentences

Practice 1

Name the underlined phrase or clause. (To review the types of phrases, see Activities 28 and 29. For clauses, see Activities 30 and 31.)

Phrases: absolute, appositive, infinitive, participial,
         past participial, prepositional

Clauses: adjective, adverb

1. <u>After the final bell</u>, he dragged himself up to the chemistry lab.

   Frank Bonham, Chief

2. One of them, <u>a tan Jersey named Blind Tillie</u>, was Cold Sassy's champion milk producer.

   Olive Ann Burns, Cold Sassy Tree

3. The immediate sight of him, <u>which should have filled them with relief and joy</u>, brought only terror.

   Richard Adams, Watership Down

4. The vampire sat back, <u>his face wearing a slight frown</u>.

   Anne Rice, Interview with the Vampire

5. <u>When he returned to the kitchen</u>, Mattie had pushed up his chair to the stove and seated herself near the lamp with a bit of sewing.

   Edith Wharton, Ethan Frome

6. He found just the right thing, <u>a little lump of sand about two feet high</u>.

   Larry McMurty, Streets of Laredo

7. <u>In the Dulancey Street area</u>, things were pretty bad.

   Jean Merrill, The Pushcart War

8. Her eyes were filled with tears, <u>watching me munch the apple</u>.
   Richard E. Kim, Lost Names

9. <u>To write good modern English</u>, you have to read modern English.
   Christy Brown, My Left Foot

10. There was a girl beside me, <u>her hands folded on her purse</u>.
    Jack Finney, "Of Missing Persons"

11. Jody ran faster then, <u>forced on by panic and rage</u>.
    John Steinbeck, The Red Pony

12. Touser roused himself under Fowler's desk and scratched another flea, <u>his leg thumping hard against the floor</u>.
    Clifford Simak, "Desertion"

13. She thought of but one thing, <u>to keep him from leaving the box</u>.
    Gaston Leroux, The Phantom of the Opera

14. Even Gurgi had been silent, <u>his eyes round with terror</u>.
    Lloyd Alexander, The Book of Three

15. <u>Filled with dissatisfaction</u>, he had slowly gone to his room and got into bed.
    Betsy Byars, The Summer of the Swans

16. The tyrannosaur was leaning against the car, <u>which rocked back and forth with each breath</u>.
    Michael Crichton, Jurassic Park

17. The tent, <u>illuminated by candle</u>, glowed warmly in the midst of the plain.
    Jack London, The Call of the Wild

18. Romey and Ima Dean and Devola, <u>who had banished themselves during the visit</u>, came around the corner of the house.
    Bill and Vera Cleaver, Where the Lilies Bloom

19. <u>Before he came to the park</u>, Harding had been the chief of veterinary medicine at the San Diego Zoo, and the world's leading expert on avian care.
    Michael Crichton, Jurassic Park

20. The dog, once huge and fleshy, but now gone to bone and covered with sores, moved in and through the house, <u>tracking mud</u>.

> *Ray Bradbury, "There Will Come Soft Rains"*

Practice 2

Each sentence is expanded in two or more places. Name the underlined phrases or clauses.

1. (A) <u>To rest</u>, (B) <u>to start over</u>, he had come west.

> *Hal Borland,* When the Legends Die

2. Rudy Warwick sat across from Dinah, (A) <u>holding one of her hands</u> and (B) <u>looking at her anxiously</u>.

> *Stephen King, "The Langoliers'"*

3. A little while later Tony climbed out on to the bank, (A) <u>his body glistening</u> and (B) <u>his hair clinging to his forehead</u>.

> *Christy Brown,* My Left Foot

4. He lived until nineteen thirty-one, (A) <u>a very old man</u>, and wrote four more books, (B) <u>which we have</u>.

> *Jack Finney, "Of Missing Persons"*

5. (A) <u>From a thousand feet</u>, (B) <u>flapping his wings</u>, he pushed over into a blazing steep dive toward the waves, and learned why seagulls don't make blazing steep power-dives.

> *Richard Bach,* Jonathan Livingston Seagull

6. (A) <u>Walking idly in the river-bed</u>, he chanced to look up and saw a donkey-cart within hailing distance, (B) <u>driven by an old man with someone else beside him</u>.

> *J. M. Coetzee,* Life and Times of Michael K

7. There was one fighter in those days, (A) <u>a pretty good light-heavyweight named Junior Ellis</u>, (B) <u>who used to sing along with country and western records before a bout</u>.

> *Robert Lipsyte,* The Contender

8. (A) <u>When Alfred went in</u>, Donatelli was standing under the single naked bulb, (B) <u>his face smooth and hard</u>.

> *Robert Lipsyte,* The Contender

9. I was close to them, (A) <u>propped up by a few pillows</u> (B) <u>against the wall</u>, (C) <u>watching</u>.

   Christy Brown, My Left Foot

10. My father, (A) <u>the Reverend Robert Fickett</u>, is a very tall, very straight man, (B) <u>who looks like what King Charles II must have looked like</u> (C) <u>when he grew older and stopped tearing around the countryside of old England</u>.

    John Neufeld, Edgar Allan

11. (A) <u>Enraged</u>, the big tyrannosaur burst from the lagoon at full speed, (B) <u>its enormous body streaming water</u>, (C) <u>as it raced up the hill past the dock</u>.

    Michael Crichton, Jurassic Park

12. Sara watched him (A) <u>as he walked</u>, (B) <u>a small figure for his ten years</u>, (C) <u>wearing faded blue jeans and a striped knit shirt that was stretched out of shape</u>.

    Betsy Byars, The Summer of the Swans

13. (A) <u>Climbing onto his pile of stones</u>, he reached up, (B) <u>his hands flat against the smooth rock</u>, (C) <u>his fingers reaching beyond his sight</u>.

    Robb White, Deathwatch

14. (A) <u>Disarmed</u>, (B) <u>stripped</u>, (C) <u>obliged to march barefoot at too fast a pace</u>, we could neither exchange our impressions nor even complain.

    Pierre Boulle, Planet of the Apes

15. They had (A) <u>to run a little</u> (B) <u>to catch up</u>, (C) <u>the poor things</u>.

    Elliott Merrick, "Without Words"

16. Simon followed at a careful distance, (A) <u>scrambling up</u>, (B) <u>hindered somewhat by the broom handle</u>, (C) <u>which he held in one hand</u>.

    Annette Curtis Klause, The Silver Kiss

17. Ima Dean, (A) <u>with a huge bag</u> (B) <u>of yellow and red wrapped candies</u>, sat on the floor, (C) <u>delving into it</u>, (D) <u>making one big pile and three smaller ones</u>.

    Bill and Vera Cleaver, Where the Lilies Bloom

18. (A) <u>At that time</u>, he was young, thin as a snake, (B) <u>with a dangerous-looking scar</u> (C) <u>over one eye</u> and (D) <u>with a few bizarre stories</u>.

Margaret Atwood, Wilderness Tips

19. For a long time he just stood there, (A) <u>defeated</u>, (B) <u>listening to the hammer</u>, (C) <u>hoping the chopper would come back</u>, but (D) <u>knowing that it would not</u>.

Robb White, Deathwatch

20. He was a broad, bandy-legged little man, (A) <u>with a walrus mustache</u>, (B) <u>with square hands</u>, (C) <u>puffed</u> and (D) <u>muscled on the palms</u>.

John Steinbeck, The Red Pony

Practice 3

Select five model sentences from Practice 1 and five from Practice 2, to imitate. Write your own content but use the structure of the model sentences.

Activity 33

Reviewing Expansions in Paragraphs

Practice 1

Name the underlined word, phrase, or clause in paragraphs one and two below. (To review the types of words, see Activity 27; phrases, see Activities 28 and 29; for clauses, see Activities 30 and 31.)

Words: single adjective or adverb

Phrases: absolute, appositive, infinitive, participial, past
        participial, prepositional

Clauses: adjective, adverb

**Paragraph One (Old House) from *The Martian Chronicles*
by Ray Bradbury**

1. (A) <u>Outside</u>, (B) <u>upon the lawn</u>, stood an iron deer.

2. (A) <u>Nearby</u>, (B) <u>on the green</u>, stood a tall brown Victorian house, (C) <u>covered with scrolls and rococo</u> (D) <u>its windows made of blue and pink and yellow and green colored glass</u>.

3. (A) <u>Upon the porch</u> were hairy geraniums and an old swing, (B) <u>which swung back and forth</u> (C) <u>in a little breeze</u>.

4. (A) <u>At the summit</u> (B) <u>of the house</u> was a cupola (C) <u>with diamond leaded-glass windows and a dunce-cap roof</u>!

5. (A) <u>Through the front window</u>, you could see a piece of music sitting on the music rest.

**Paragraph Two (Dinosaur) from "A Sound of Thunder"
by Ray Bradbury**

1. It towered thirty feet above half of the trees, (A) <u>a great evil god</u>, (B) <u>folding its delicate watchmaker's claws close to its oily reptilian chest</u>.

2. Each lower leg was a piston, (A) <u>covered in thick ropes of muscle</u>, (B) <u>sheathed over in a gleam of pebbled skin like the mail of a terrible warrior</u>.

3. (A) <u>From the great breathing cage</u> (B) <u>of the upper body</u>, those two delicate arms dangled out front, (C) <u>those arms with hands</u> (D) <u>which might pick up and examine men like toys</u>, (E) <u>while the snake neck coiled</u>.

4. The head itself, (A) <u>a ton of sculptured stone</u>, lifted easily upon the sky.

5. Its mouth gaped, (A) <u>exposing a fence of teeth like daggers</u>.

6. Its eyes rolled, (A) <u>ostrich eggs</u>, (B) <u>empty</u> of all expression save hunger.

7. It ran, (A) <u>its pelvic bones crushing aside trees and buses</u>, (B) <u>its taloned feet clawing damp earth</u>, (C) <u>leaving prints six inches deep wherever it settled its weight</u>.

8. It ran with a gliding ballet step, (A) <u>poised</u> and (B) <u>balanced for all its ten tons</u>.

9. It moved into a sunlit arena warily, (A) <u>its beautifully reptile hands feeling the air</u>.

Practice 2

Name the underlined word, phrase, or clause in paragraphs three and four below. Then write imitations of those paragraphs. Expand your sentences in the same places and in the same way as in the model paragraphs.

Paragraph Three (Motorcycle Crash) from "Cyclists' Raid" by Frank Rooney

1. The motorcycle on the sidewalk speeded up and skidded obliquely into a plate-glass window, (A) <u>its front wheels bucking and climbing the brick base beneath the window</u>.

2. A single large section of glass slipped edge-down to the sidewalk and fell slowly toward the cyclist (A) <u>who backed</u>

clumsily away from it, (B) his feet spread and kicking at the cement.

Paragraph Four (Pony) from *The Red Pony* by John Steinbeck

1. Every morning, (A) after Jody had curried and brushed the pony, he let down the barrier of the stall, and the pony thrust past him and raced down the barn and into the corral.

2. (A) Around and (B) around, he galloped, and sometimes he jumped forward and landed (C) on stiff legs.

3. He stood quivering, (A) his stiff ears forward, (B) eyes rolling so that the whites showed, (C) pretending to be frightened.

4. (A) At last, he walked to the water-trough, (B) snorting loudly, and buried his nose in the water up to the nostrils.

Practice 3

Expand paragraphs five and six below. Use the type of phrase or clause listed after Expansions. To get you started, the beginning words are provided. When you finish, compare your sentences to the sentences by the professional writers in the References section. Also, to familiarize yourself with how professionals write, copy the sentences.

Paragraph Five (Death of a Vampire) from *Salem's Lot* by Stephen King

1. Blood splashed upward in a cold gush, blinding . . .

   Expansions: present participial phrase

2. The mouth widened gapingly as . . . , meeting . . . and disappearing . . .

   Expansions: adverb clause, present participial phrase, present participial phrase

3. The fingernails went black and peeled off, and then there were only bones, dressed . . . , clicking and clenching . . .

Expansions: past participial phrase, present participial phrase, present participial phrase

4. Dust puffed <u>through</u> . . .

   Expansions: prepositional phrase

5. The pants, <u>with</u> . . . <u>to fill</u> . . . , fell away to broomsticks clad in black silk.

   Expansions: prepositional phrase, infinitive phrase

Paragraph Six (Touchdown) from "The Eighty-Yard Run" by Irwin Shaw

1. The pass was high and wide and Darling jumped for it, <u>feeling</u> . . .

   Expansions: present participial phrase

2. The center floated by, <u>his hands</u> . . . <u>as Darling</u> . . .

   Expansions: absolute phrase, adverb clause

3. He had ten yards in the clear and picked up speed, <u>breathing</u> . . . , <u>feeling</u> . . . , <u>listening</u> . . . , <u>pulling</u> . . . , <u>watching</u> . . .

   Expansions: series of five present participial phrases

4. He smiled a little to himself <u>as he</u> . . . , <u>holding</u> . . . , <u>his knees</u> . . . , <u>his hips</u> . . .

   Expansions: adverb clause, present participial phrase, absolute phrase, absolute phrase

5. The first halfback came at him, and he fed him his leg, then swung at the last moment, took the shock of the man's shoulder without breaking stride, ran through him, <u>his cleats</u> . . .

   Expansions: absolute phrase

6. There was only the safety man now, <u>coming</u> . . . , <u>his arms</u> . . . , <u>his hands</u> . . .

   Expansions: present participial phrase, absolute phrase, absolute phrase

7. Darling tucked the ball in, spurted at him, <u>driving</u> . . . , <u>hurling</u> . . . , <u>his legs</u> . . . , <u>his knees</u> . . . , <u>all two hundred pounds of him</u> . . .

   Expansions: present participial phrase, present participial phrase, absolute phrase, absolute phrase, absolute phrase

8. He was sure he was going <u>to get</u> . . .

   Expansions: infinitive phrase

9. <u>Without</u> . . . , <u>his arms and legs</u> . . . , he headed right for the safety man and stiff-armed him, <u>feeling</u> . . . , <u>seeing</u> . . . , <u>with</u> . . .

   Expansions: prepositional phrase, absolute phrase, present participial phrase, present participial phrase, prepositional phrase

10. He pivoted away, <u>keeping</u> . . . , <u>dropping</u> . . . <u>as he</u> . . . .

    Expansions: participial phrase, participial phrase, adverb clause

In this last sentence, the runner, a professional football player, scored a touchdown, and you, having learned how professionals write their sentences, achieved a major goal in significant writing improvement. Congratulations!

References
Activity 1
Understanding Sentence Parts

Practice 1:
2

Practice 2:
1. b
2. b
3. b
4. a
5. b
6. a
7. b
8. a
9. b
10. b

Activity 2
Identifying Sentence Parts

Practice 1:
Answers may vary. Here are some possibilities for meaningful divisions of sentence parts.

1. When fate / hands you a lemon / try to make lemonade.

2. Even if it's a little thing / do something for others / something for which / you get no pay / but the privilege of doing it.
3. The best way / to cheer yourself up / is to try / to cheer somebody else up.
4. A sentence should contain no unnecessary words / a paragraph no unnecessary sentences / for the same reason / that a drawing should have no unnecessary lines / and a machine no unnecessary parts.
5. Always be nice to people / on the way up / because you'll meet the same people / on the way down.
6. When you have a number / of disagreeable duties / to perform / always do / the most disagreeable first.
7. Keep five yards from a carriage / ten yards from a horse / and a hundred yards from an elephant / but the distance you should keep from a wicked person / cannot be measured.
8. Ask not / what your country can do for you / but ask what you / can do for your country.
9. You can make more friends in two months / by becoming interested in other people / than you can in two years / by trying to get other people / interested in you.
10. If you wish to rest / first work.

Practice 2:
Answers will vary.

Activity 3
Understanding Sentence Unscrambling

Practice 1:
2

Practice 2:
List 1: When the ashtray, which was solid and feathered with grease, sang for him the dance of the petunia and became encouraged to jump up to an ocean and hope for mud, the crab blanked its pencil and covered the floor with its pizzas.

List 2: Although the hamburger, which was crystal and demented in town, ran down to him the story of the onion and seemed reluctant to fly away in a dictionary and study for words, the bun opened its halves and embraced the cheese in an instant.

Activity 4
Unscrambling Sentence Parts

Practice 1:

1. At the foot of one of the trees, the boy's father sat, the lantern still burning by his side.

2. The father was respectable and tight, a mortgage financier and a stern, upright collection-plate passer and forecloser.

3. After Buck Fanshaw's inquest, a meeting of the short-haired brotherhood was held, for nothing can be done on the Pacific coast without a public meeting and an expression of sentiment.

4. With them, carrying a gnarled walking stick, was Elmo Goodhue Pipgrass, the littlest, oldest man I had ever seen.

5. He bounded out of bed wearing a long flannel nightgown over long woolen underwear, a nightcap, and a leather jacket around his chest.

6. Once upon a sunny morning a man who sat in a breakfast nook looked up from his scrambled eggs to see a white unicorn with a gold horn quietly cropping the roses in the garden.

7. Then, out of a box on the bed, she removed the gleaming pair of patent-leather dancing pumps, grabbed my right foot, and shoved it into one of them, using her finger as a shoehorn.

8. As a general rule, careful on-the-scene investigations disclose that most "unidentified" flying objects are quite ordinary phenomena, such as weather balloons, meteorites, satellites, and even once a man named Lewis Mandelbaum, who blew off the roof of the World Trade Center.

9. The barnyard sounds that we heard escaped from two crates of hens that the Duvitches had fetched along and from a burlap bag in which a small flock of ducks had been stowed.

10. I was fourteen years of age when a coward going by the name of Tom Chaney shot my father down in Fort Smith, Arkansas, and robbed him of his life and his horse and $150 in cash money plus two California gold pieces that he carried in his trouser band.

Practice 2:
Answers will vary.

Activity 5
Unscrambling Paragraphs

Practice 1:
Then it moved around the side of the car. The big raised tail blocked their view out of all the side windows. At the back the animal snorted, a deep rumbling growl that blended with the thunder. It sank its jaws into the spare tire mounted on the back of the Land Cruiser and, in a single head shake, tore it away. The rear of the car lifted into the air for a moment, and then it thumped down with a muddy splash.

Practice 2:
As if in the superhuman energy of his utterance there had been found the potency of a spell, the huge antique panels to which the speaker pointed threw slowly back, upon the instant, their ponderous and ebony jaws. It was the work of the rushing gust— but then without those doors there *did* stand the lofty and enshrouded figure of the Lady Madeline of Usher. There was blood upon her white robes, and the evidence of some bitter struggle upon every portion of her emaciated frame. For a moment she remained trembling and reeling to and fro upon the threshold—then, with a low, moaning cry, fell heavily inward upon the person of her brother, and in her violent and now final death-agonies, bore him to the floor a corpse, and a victim to the terrors he had anticipated.

Activity 6
Avoiding Comma Splices

Practice 1:
1. Comma splice is between e and f.
2. Comma splice is between b and c.
3. Comma splice is between c and d.
4. Comma splice is between g and h.

Practice 2:
1. products, the
2. health, his
3. it, I

4. itself, the

5. bearers, his

Activity 7
Identifying and Removing Comma Splices

Practice 1:

1. Comma splice is between c and d.

2. Comma splice is between d and e.

3. Comma splice is between d and e.

4. Comma splice is between h and i.

Practice 2:
(2), (6), (13), (16), (21)

Activity 8
Varying Sentence Structure

Practice 1:
Answers will vary.

Practice 2:
Changes will vary.

Activity 9
Matching Sentence Structures

Practice 1:

1. The class scattered in all directions, running.

2. When the winner appeared, the crowd started to shout louder and louder in the stadium.

3. Refreshed, feeling tremendous relief from pressure and performance, in a mood much improved because of vacation, he started to swing his tennis racket.

4. He spoke one slow, nervous sentence, like a friend who has often been hurt and believes that expressions of honesty now must be guarded.

5. Prom dancers spun around in the gym during the last dance that night, stomping loudly, their arms up, their bodies swaying, the band blaring. (Some sentence parts may acceptably be interchanged.)

Practice 2:
Nonsense versions may acceptably interchange some sentence parts.

1. Bob wrote his song, rehearsed it in the evenings, sang it beautifully in the play, but the small orchestra played with the beat ahead of the singer.
2. Snaze kurped its blander, broded it with the snart, crassed it frinkly from the marton, and the plimey peesto scrunted in the tunert of a bleepert.
3. To bring work from the office is to "relax" in a state of constant worry.
4. To jeld crams near town is to murd in a zipple from a zapple.
5. A sportscaster who communicates with fans and sports' top athletes is the choice announcer who communicates with great enthusiasm and with solid knowledge.
6. The blends which croak from selfhoose and their brained nabort are the best blends which croak near thirty bleeps and near forty bloops.
7. The wrinkled skin, very dry, yet with a softness about it as appealing as the sparkle in Grandma's eyes, shone in the candlelight.
8. An oversized saltert, quite pritert, and of a color on it as lumrious as a klanion in its woostem, plazoned from a yambrod.

Activity 10
Identifying Sentence Imitations

Practice 1:
Answers will vary.

Practice 2:
1. a and c
2. a and c
3. a and c
4. a and b

Activity 11
Identifying Models and Imitations

Practice 1:

1. b and h

2. e and g

3. c and f

4. a and d

Practice 2:
Answers will vary.

Activity 12
Learning How to Imitate Sentences

Practice 1:

1. Levon and James stood together in the hallway, sorting through the heap on the floor of books, notebooks, loose pages, pens, and pencils.

2. Appearing in a nearby doorway was the menacing shadow of their homeroom teacher.

3. On the floor below them was Levon's bookbag strewn open from the fall, and scattered there the debris that he had dropped just seconds before.

4. Levon bent his body toward the floor, and then knelt there, his hands vacuuming the contents into the bookbag, his face hidden from the stare of his teacher in the doorway.

Practice 2:
Imitations will vary.

Activity 13
Imitating Sentence Variety (Part One)

Practice 1:
Imitations will vary.

Practice 2:
Responses will vary.

Activity 14
Imitating Sentence Variety (Part Two)

Practice 1:
Imitations will vary.

Practice 2:
Responses will vary.

Activity 15
Imitating Sentences in Paragraphs

Practice 2:
Imitations will vary.

Activity 16
Imitating Long Sentences

Practice 1:
All sentence parts, except the last, begin with *when*.

Practice 2:
Imitations will vary.

Activity 17
Imitating Paragraphs (Part One)

Practice 1:
Paragraphs three, four, and six are the imitations.

Practice 2:
Imitations will vary.

Activity 18
Imitating Paragraphs (Part Two)

Practice 1:
Notice that most sentences have the verb before the subject.

Practice 2:
Imitations will vary.

Activity 19
Imitating an Introductory Paragraph

Practice 1:
Notice that most sentences contain a brief phrase that identifies the person interviewed.

Practice 2:
Responses will vary. Successful reports will have sentences that resemble the kind of sentences in professional writing, not just the imitation sentences based upon the sentences in the model paragraph.

Activity 20
Imitating Professional Opening Paragraphs

Practice 1:
Imitations will vary.

Practice 2:
All sentences, not just the imitation sentence, should resemble the kind of sentences in professional writing.

Activity 21
Decombining Sentences

Practice 1:
Responses will vary.

Practice 2:
Responses will vary.

Practice 3:
Responses will vary.

Activity 22
Combining Then Imitating

Practice 1: (These are the originals.)
1. Abruptly, they burst out of the clouds into a shaft of light.

2. She was in the doorway, excited and afraid.

3. Hungry, Thomas ate two portions of meat, nothing else.

4. Warily, slowly, he began to angle toward the valley.

5. He was a mean-looking man, red in the face and bearded.

6. To hide the tears, he lowered his eyes.

7. He ate slowly, hoping that in days to come he'd be able to remember how good each mouthful had been.

8. In the spring of 1940, the birds migrated early from the Great Marsh.

9. Totally dismayed by what had happened, he then buried his face in his hands and cried.

10. The meat, dry-cured for the feeding of the dogs, hung in the smoke-house.

11. Gwydion, whose eyes were everywhere at once, caught sight of them instantly.

12. She rose from the table, where she was sitting.

13. By afternoon, Perrault, who was in a hurry to be on the trail to Dawson, returned with three more dogs.

14. When Fiver said the iron tree was harmless, they believed him.

15. He looked like the total all-American kid as he pedaled his twenty-six-inch Schwinn with the apehanger handlebars up the residential suburban street. (No comma needed.)

Practice 2:

1. Aunt Dorothy, tall and bony, was waiting at the front door with her own small daughter, Diane.

2. In the dining hall, over the stone fireplace that was never used, there was a huge moulting stuffed moose head, which looked somehow carnivorous.

3. Calm now, at peace, Craig sat and waited for his father to tell him what he should do next, just as he had done so many times as a child.

4. Perhaps an elderly gentleman lived there, alone, someone who had known her grandfather, someone who had visited the Parrs in Cummington.

5. In the closed anteroom, the lawyer lay on an old Army cot he kept there for naps, a newspaper folded over his face as though he were a corpse being protected from flies.

Activity 23
Combining Effectively

Practice 1:

1a. The boy watched, his eyes bulging in the dark.
      Edmund Ware, "An Underground Episode"

2b. One of the dogs, the best one, had disappeared.
      Fred Gipson, Old Yeller

3a. The country house, on this particular wintry afternoon, was most enjoyable.
      James Thurber, "The Owl in the Attic"

4b. The dying animal snarled, and suddenly lifted its head and twisted, sinking its teeth into the neck of its attacker.
      Michael Crichton, Jurassic Park

5a. Men slept in bunks or hammocks so tightly squeezed together that the reclining bodies looked like slabs of meat packed for the market wagons.
      William Styron, A Tidewater Morning

Practice 2:

1. He moves nervously and fast, but with a restraint that suggests that he is a cautious, thoughtful man.
      John Hersey, Hiroshima

2. The girls stood aside, talking among themselves, looking over their shoulders at the boys, and the very small children rolled in the dust or clung to the hands of their older brothers or sisters.

Shirley Jackson, "The Lottery"

3. He took flour and oil, shaped a cake in a frying pan, and lighted the little stove that functioned on bottled gas.

Albert Camus, "The Guest"

4. When the cake was done, he set it on the windowsill to cool, heated some condensed milk diluted with water, and beat up the eggs into an omelette.

Albert Camus, "The Guest"

5. The fifth traveler, a withered old gentleman sitting next to the middle door across the aisle, napped fitfully upon his cane.

Henry Sydnor Harrison, "Miss Hinch"

Practice 3:
Answers will vary.

Activity 24
Combining Economically

Practice 1:

1. Now the sky was without a cloud, pale blue, delicate, luminous, scintillating with morning.

2. From ten to fifteen he distributed handbills for merchants, held horses, and ran confidential errands.

3. Nick looked down into clear, brown water, colored from the pebbly bottom, and watched the trout keeping themselves steady in the current with wavering fins.

4. On one side, beginning at the very lip of the pool, was a tiny meadow, a cool, resilient surface of green that extended to the base of the browning wall.

5. He turned on the TV, found a Cincinnati-Boston exhibition baseball game wending its slow way into the eighth inning, lay down on the sofa to watch it, and almost immediately dozed off.

Practice 2:
Answers will vary.

Activity 25
Combining Sentences in Paragraphs

Practice 1:
(1) This is a snail shell, round, full, and glossy as a horse chestnut. (2) Comfortable and compact, it sits curled up in the hollow of my hand like a cat. (3) Milky and opaque, it has the pinkish bloom of the sky on a summer evening, ripening to rain. (4) On its smooth symmetrical face is pencilled with precision a spiral, winding inward to the pinpoint center of the shell, the tiny dark core of the apex, the pupil of the eye. (5) It stares at me, this mysterious eye, and I stare back.

(1) Manuel, leaning against the barrera, watching the bull, waved his hand, and the gypsy ran out, trailing his cape. (2) The bull, in full gallop, pivoted and charged the cape, his head down, his tail rising. (3) The gypsy moved in a zigzag, and as he passed, the bull caught sight of him and abandoned the cape to charge the man. (4) The gypsy sprinted and vaulted the red fence of the barrera as the bull struck it with his horns. (5) He tossed into it twice with his horns, banging into the wood blindly.

Practice 2:
(1) Outside, upon this lawn, stood an iron deer. (2) Further up on the green stood a tall brown Victorian house, quiet in the sunlight, all covered with scrolls and rococo, its windows made of blue and pink and yellow and green colored glass. (3) Upon the porch were hairy geraniums and an old swing which was hooked into the porch ceiling and which now swung back and forth, back and forth, in a little breeze. (4) At the summit of the house was a cupola with diamond leaded-glass windows and a dunce-cap roof!

(1) Ulrich von Gradwitz found himself stretched on the ground, one arm numb beneath him and the other held almost as helplessly in a tight tangle of forked branches, while both legs were pinned beneath the fallen mass. (2) His heavy shooting boots had saved his feet from being crushed to pieces, but if his fractures were not as serious as they might have been, at least it was evident that he could not move from his present position till someone came to release him. (3) The descending twigs had slashed the skin of his face, and he had to wink away some drops of blood from his eyelashes before he could take in a general view of the disaster. (4) At his side, so near that under ordinary circumstances he could

almost have touched him, lay Georg Znaeym, alive and struggling but obviously as helplessly pinioned down as himself. (5) All round them lay a thick-strewn wreckage of splintered branches and broken twigs.

Activity 26
Combining to Revise

Practice 1:
Results will vary.

Practice 2:
Results will vary.

Activity 27
Expanding with Words

Practice 1:
Imitations will vary.

Practice 2:

1. The man was about fifty, <u>overweight</u> but <u>solid-looking</u>.

2. <u>Outside</u>, the gust of wind threw sand against the car.

3. Templeton, <u>asleep</u> in the straw, heard the commotion and awoke.

4. Bea is a fine-looking woman, <u>plump</u> and <u>firm</u> still, with rich brown skin and thick black hair.

5. We all remembered someone, and I remembered my father, so <u>tall</u> and <u>strong</u> and <u>kind</u>.

6. Laughter, <u>loud</u> and <u>warm</u> from their long and intimate relationship, filled the room.

7. <u>Miserable</u> and <u>disconsolate</u>, he wandered about the many tents, only to find that one place was as cold as another.

8. <u>On</u> and <u>on</u>, they drove through the darkness, and though the rain stopped, the wind rushed by and whistled and made strange sounds.

9. Hattie sat down at her old Spanish table, watching them in the cloudy warmth of the day, clasping her hands, <u>chuckling</u> and <u>sad</u>.

10. Beyond Romey's slight figure I saw this tree, <u>alone</u> and <u>different</u> from the rest, its branches all streamed back in one direction from the winds that had battered it year after year.

Activity 28
Expanding with Phrases (Part One)

Practice 1:
Imitations will vary.

Practice 2:

1. <u>A short, round boy of seven</u>, he took little interest in troublesome things, preferring to remain on good terms with everyone. (appositive phrase)

2. I looked out across the ravaged fields and saw Romey, <u>a vaporous figure in the distance</u>, moving around in Roy Luther's garden. (appositive phrase)

3. The real estate agent, <u>an old man with a smiling, hypocritical face</u>, soon joined them. (appositive phrase)

4. There they were in the schoolroom again, <u>the five boys and Lina and the teacher</u>. (series of appositive phrases)

5. I could see Lestat feeling along the brick walls, <u>his hard enduring vampire face a twisted mask of human frustration</u>. (absolute phrase)

6. On impulse, he went in, bought a bag of gumdrops, and went on up the street, <u>his mouth full of candy</u>. (absolute phrase)

7. Slowly, <u>his muscles flexing tightly against his thin shirt</u> and <u>his sweat popping off his skin like oil on water</u>, he lifted the truck in one fluid, powerful motion unil the front was several inches off the ground and slowly walked it to the left of the road, where he set it down as gently as a sleeping child. (series of absolute phrases)

8. <u>To be sure</u>, he lowered his head, resting it against the wall and reached up with his hands, feeling all over the stone above him. (infinitive phrase)

9. Slowly, I crawled on, stopping to listen, <u>to glance back, to measure the distance between me and the spring</u>. (series of infinitive phrases)

10. He knew the bears would soon be leaving their winter dens, <u>to travel</u>, <u>to claim their old ranges</u>, <u>to challenge intruders</u>, and <u>to fight their fearful battles among themselves</u>. (series of infinitive phrases)

Activity 29
Expanding with Phrases (Part Two)

Practice 1:
Imitations will vary.

Practice 2:
1. <u>Upon a stage</u>, a woman sang. (prepositional phrase)

2. <u>Around the fiery circle</u>, warriors on high stilts beat upraised swords against their shields. (prepositional phrase)

3. <u>Across the stalk land, into the pine woods, into the climbing, brightening glow of the dawn</u>, the boy followed the dog, whose anxious pace slowed from age as they went. (series of prepositional phrases)

4. Mary asked no more questions but waited in the darkness of her corner, <u>keeping her eyes on the window</u>. (participial phrase)

5. A large woman, <u>wearing faded overalls</u>, got out and waddled over to them. (participial phrase)

6. Ima Dean, with a huge bag of yellow and red wrapped candies, was sitting on the floor, <u>delving into it</u>, <u>making one big pile and three smaller ones</u>. (series of participial phrases)

7. They were standing there in front of the locked door in the nearly empty plane, <u>laughing wildly</u>, when the man in the red shirt and the man in the crew-necked jersey arrived,

looking at them as if they had both gone crazy. (two participial phrases in different places)

8. He walked on, <u>surrounded by skipping, laughing children</u>. (past participial phrase)

9. <u>Crumpled there</u>, he held his temples desperately with both hands and was wretchedly sick. (past participial phrase)

10. He was a broad, bandy-legged little man with a walrus mustache, with square hands, <u>puffed and muscled on the palms</u>. (series of past participial phrases)

Activity 30
Expanding with Clauses (Part One)

Practice 1:
Imitations will vary.

Practice 2:

1. Red, <u>who had called Meo a hero who wound up broke</u>, was the one who died penniless.

2. They had planned to spend the first night at Bardstown, <u>which in good weather was only a few hours away down in Kentucky</u>.

3. She also had to watch our three chickens, <u>which loved to wander away from our farm</u>.

4. Boysie, <u>who slept in the kitchen</u>, heard the door shut and came to the living room.

5. Ramo was standing on one foot and then the other, watching the ship coming, <u>which he did not know was a ship</u>.

Activity 31
Expanding with Clauses (Part Two)

Practice 1:
Imitations will vary.

Practice 2:

1. We passed two children, sobbing and moaning <u>as they ran</u>.

2. <u>After Uncle Daniels had finished with his lambchop dinner</u>, I set the cream puffs on the coffee table and stood back looking at them.

3. In the winter, <u>when everything's frozen</u>, I hate the mountains.

4. Dicey was up and dressed, washed and fed, and out the door, with the day's work outlined in her head, <u>before anyone else stirred in the silent house</u>.

5. <u>When kernel-picking time came</u>, <u>before it was dark each day</u>, the boy or the father took a hammer with a homemade handle, went to the flat rock, and cracked as many walnuts as could be kerneled in a night. (two adverb clauses)

Activity 32
Reviewing Expansions in Sentences

Practice 1:

1. prepositional phrase

2. appositive phrase

3. adjective clause

4. absolute phrase

5. adverb clause

6. appositive phrase

7. prepositional phrase

8. participial phrase

9. infinitive phrase

10. absolute phrase

11. past participial phrase

12. absolute phrase

13. infinitive phrase

14. absolute phrase

15. past participial phrase

16. adjective clause

17. past participial phrase

18. adjective clause

19. adverb clause

20. participial phrase

Practice 2:

1. (A) infinitive phrase, (B) infinitive phrase

2. (A) participial phrase, (B) participial phrase

3. (A) absolute phrase, (B) absolute phrase

4. (A) appositive phrase, (B) adjective clause

5. (A) prepositional phrase, (B) participial phrase

6. (A) participial phrase, (B) past participial phrase

7. (A) appositive phrase, (B) adjective clause

8. (A) adverb clause, (B) absolute phrase

9. (A) past participial phrase, (B) prepositional phrase, (C) participial phrase

10. (A) appositive phrase, (B) adjective clause, (C) adverb clause

11. (A) past participial phrase, (B) absolute phrase, (C) adverb clause

12. (A) adverb clause, (B) appositive phrase, (C) participial phrase

13. (A) participial phrase, (B) absolute phrase, (C) absolute phrase

14. (A) past participial phrase, (B) past participial phrase, (C) past participial phrase

15. (A) infinitive phrase, (B) infinitive phrase, (C) appositive phrase

16. (A) particpial phrase, (B) past participial phrase, (C) adjective clause.

17. (A) prepositional phrase, (B) prepositional phrase, (C) participial phrase, (D) participial phrase

18. (A) prepositional phrase, (B) prepositional phrase, (C) prepositional phrase, (D) prepositional phrase

19. (A) past participial phrase, (B) participial phrase, (C) participial phrase, (D) participial phrase

20. (A) prepositional phrase, (B) prepositional phrase, (C) past participial phrase, (D) past participial phrase

Practice 3:
Imitations will vary.

Activity 33
Reviewing Expansions in Paragraphs

Practice 1:
Paragraph One

1. (A) adverb, (B) prepositional phrase

2. (A) adverb, (B) prepositional phrase, (C) past participial phrase, (D) absolute phrase

3. (A) prepositional phrase, (B) adjective clause, (C) prepositional phrase

4. (A) prepositional phrase, (B) prepositional phrase, (C) prepositional phrase

5. (A) prepositional phrase

Paragraph Two

1. (A) appositive phrase, (B) participial phrase

2. (A) past participial phrase, (B) past participial phrase

3. (A) prepositional phrase, (B) prepositional phrase, (C) appositive phrase, (D) adjective clause, (E) adverb clause

4. (A) appositive phrase

5. (A) participial phrase

6. (A) appositive phrase, (B) adjective

7. (A) absolute phrase, (B) absolute phrase, (C) participial phase

8. (A) past participial phrase, (B) past participial phrase

9. (A) absolute phrase

Practice 2:
Paragraph Three

1. (A) absolute phrase

2. (A) adjective clause, (B) absolute phrase

Paragraph Four

1. (A) adverb clause

2. (A) adverb, (B) adverb, (C) prepositional phrase

3. (A) absolute phrase, (B) absolute phrase, (C) participial phrase

4. (A) prepositional phrase, (B) participial phrase

Practice 3:
Paragraph Five

1. Blood splashed upward in a cold gush, <u>blinding the vampire momentarily</u>.

2. The mouth widened gapingly <u>as the lips drew back and drew back</u>, <u>meeting the nose</u> and <u>disappearing in an oral ring of jutting teeth</u>.

3. The fingernails went black and peeled off, and then there were only bones, <u>dressed still with rings</u>, <u>clicking</u> and <u>clenching like castanets</u>.

4. Dust puffed <u>through its linen shirt</u>.

5. The pants, <u>with nothing to fill them out</u>, fell away to broomsticks clad in black silk.

Paragraph Six

1. The pass was high and wide and Darling jumped for it, <u>feeling it slap flatly against his hands as he shook his hips to throw off the halfback who was diving at him</u>.

2. The center floated by, <u>his hands desperately brushing Darling's knee as Darling picked his feet up high and delicately ran over a blocker and an opposing linesman in a jumble on the ground near the scrimmage line</u>.

3. He had ten yards in the clear and picked up speed, <u>breathing easily</u>, <u>feeling his thighpads rising and falling against his legs</u>, <u>listening to the sound of cleats behind him</u>, <u>pulling away from them</u>, <u>watching the other backs heading him off toward the sideline, the men closing in on him, and the blockers fighting for position</u>.

4. He smiled a little to himself <u>as he ran</u>, <u>holding the ball lightly in front of him with his two hands</u>, <u>his knees pumping high</u>, <u>his hips twisting in the almost girlish run of a back in a broken field</u>.

5. The first halfback came at him, and he fed him his leg, then swung at the last moment, took the shock of the man's shoulder without breaking stride, ran through him, <u>his cleats biting securely into the turf</u>.

6. There was only the safety man now, <u>coming warily at him</u>, <u>his arms crooked</u>, <u>his hands spread</u>.

7. Darling tucked the ball in, spurted at him, <u>driving hard</u>, <u>hurling himself along</u>, <u>his legs pounding</u>, <u>his knees high</u>, <u>all two hundred pounds of him bunched into controlled attack</u>.

8. He was sure he was going <u>to get past the safety man</u>.

9. <u>Without thought,</u> <u>his arms and legs working beautifully</u>
   <u>together,</u> he headed right for the safety man and stiff-armed
   him, <u>feeling blood spurt instantaneously from the man's</u>
   <u>nose onto his hand,</u> <u>seeing his face go awry,</u> <u>with his head</u>
   <u>turned and his mouth pulled to one side</u>.

10. He pivoted away, <u>keeping the arm locked,</u> <u>dropping the</u>
    <u>safety man</u> <u>as he ran easily toward the goal line</u>.